Just Moms

Conveying Justice in an Unjust World

stories compiled by

Melanie Springer Mock

and

Rebekah D. Schneiter

BARCLAY PRESS
Newberg, OR 97132

JUST MOMS
Conveying Justice in an Unjust World
edited by Melanie Springer Mock and Rebekah D. Schneiter

© 2011 by Barclay Press

BARCLAY PRESS
Newberg, OR
www.barclaypress.com

Scripture quotations marked "ESV" are taken from *The Holy Bible, English Standard Version*. Copyright © 2000; 2001 by Crossway Bibles, a division of Good News Publishers. Used by permission. All rights reserved.

Scripture quotations marked "NLT" are taken from the *Holy Bible, New Living Translation*, copyright 1996, 2004. Used by permission of Tyndale House Publishers, Inc., Wheaton, Illinois 60189. All rights reserved.

Scripture quotations marked "NIV" are taken from *The Holy Bible, New International Version*®, NIV® Copyright © 1973, 1978, 1984, 2010 by Biblica, Inc.™ Used by permission. All rights reserved worldwide.

Scripture marked "NKJV" taken from the New King James Version. Copyright © 1982 by Thomas Nelson, Inc. Used by permission. All rights reserved.

CREDITS

"Wealth Isn't in the Crayons" by Dorcas Smucker is reprinted from *Downstairs the Queen Is Knitting* © by Good Books (www.GoodBooks.com). Used by permission. All rights reserved.

"Knowing Place" by Lee Snyder was originally published in *At Powerline and Diamond Hill* © by Cascadia Publishing House and is used here with permission.

COVER DESIGN BY DARRYL BROWN

ISBN 978-1-59498-022-0

Contents

Blessed Are the Peacemakers

Lilies of the Field

In the World

Alphabetical list of writers

Introduction

MY SECOND SON, Coen, is quite passionate. This made for some crazy "terrible twos." But his passion is turning out to be a good character trait. Coen feels everything—joy, anticipation, anger, frustration, injustice—and so I think he also feels the presence of Jesus more acutely than do others. The other day we were talking about Jesus and how we believe him even though we don't see him. Coen stated, "Jesus sleeps with me in my bed." And you know, I think he does. When I listen to Coen's prayers I realize he is in a relationship with his God — who evidently slumbers on the second floor of our farmhouse.

Over spring break our feisty three-year-old noticed someone the rest of us didn't. As we sat eating our pizza on the brick steps of Portland's Pioneer Courthouse Square, everyone seemed oblivious to the hungry man to our left. Except for Coen. I caught him scooting his plate of pizza toward this man, who was clearly living on the streets. The man seemed uncomfortable taking food from a child; I would be too.

I intervened, "Coen, are you wanting to give that man your pizza?"

"Yes."

I wanted to shout to everyone in downtown Portland: "Did you see that? Did you see my amazing son? He acted out on the prompting of God; he gave his food to someone in need! He gets it."

Later when I asked Coen why he gave his pizza away, he stated simply, "Because he didn't have any."

Of course, just when I think parenting is going really well, something backfires. Like when we were driving home from our trip into Portland and Coen refused to give one fruit snack to his younger brother. I'm not going to share this particular mothering triumph with my friends, or post an update on Facebook about my son's inability to share.

But maybe I should. Maybe that is exactly what my friend at the indoor park needs to hear: that she's normal, her child is normal, and her child's current state is okay. I'm learning to hold my children's choices and actions loosely, for they mirror my own walk with God—a rocky, cyclical journey that ebbs and flows with obedience and disobedience, confidence and insecurity. For all of us, parenting is an act of faith and trust. We trust the process. We trust that the Spirit of God is at work through our shining moments and through our failures. And sometimes, we look to others for guidance, commiseration, and a sense that we are in this parenting work together—recognizing that a community of other parents can provide meaning to our efforts.

I hope you will find such a community in this book, *Just Moms*. We offer no easy solution to the hard task of teaching our children to live a selfless life; this is not a how-to guide, and you will not find here any step-by-step approaches to how one might teach peace or justice. Instead, we have gathered stories from mothers doing their very best to convey values to their children. The stories in this book celebrate successes and describe failures, reflecting both our varied approaches to parenting and the variable responses our children give to even our most concerted efforts. We have included, too, the voices of parents from across the spectrum of experience: from those whose children are still young, to those struggling with teenagers swept up by the complexity of adolescence, to mothers with grown children who now see the fruit of their years-long labor.

The Friends (Quaker) tradition recognizes the significance of community in helping each other to affirm the Light within. Our intent is that this book can, in its own way, call us to such a community, bringing the reality of the kingdom of heaven here on earth. In telling our own stories of parenting, we hope to encourage others to tell theirs, and together we can find ways to uphold what is right and good. Perhaps most significantly, we hope in telling our stories we will acknowledge the movement of God in everyone: in ourselves, when we are at our best and worst as parents; in each other, when we are struggling to do right by our children and our faith; and in our children, both when they are embracing peace by sharing pizza with a homeless man or showing complete selfishness, failing to share just one fruit snack with a screaming baby brother.

Rebekah Schneiter
August 2010

All One in Christ Jesus

"There is neither Jew nor Greek,
there is neither slave nor free,
there is no male and female,
for you are all one in Christ Jesus."

Galatians 3:28 ESV

His Pink Shoes

Amy Lutz

Amy Lutz lives in Newberg, Oregon, in a house overrun with males—her husband; two sons, Truman (9) and Asher (6); a dog; and two cats.

As assistant professor of education at George Fox University, Amy loves fostering the writing teacher inside each of her students. When she taught middle school she utilized her innate goofiness to inspire her young students to find their writing voice.

She holds out hope that the family's pet lizards are female to gain some sisterhood in the house.

ASHER DISPLAYS his personal style without reservation. He thinks nothing of wearing mismatched rain boots and a firefighter's hat to his brother's baseball game, or Batman pajamas (with cape) and cowboy boots for berry picking. Once, he wore full western gear with a sheriff's badge for a play date at McDonald's.

He's fearless that way.

I love it.

Rhythmical tides, outside the Puget Sound beach house we shared with friends, beckoned us to a weekend of endless exploration. From boat rides on waist-high water to sand-dollar excavation in the muddy bottoms, it was a perfect playland for our kids. Prepared, I packed clothes, extra clothes, and rubber boots. Within an hour of our arrival Asher had muddied his lot. But our host—one of those mothers who thinks of everything— pulled out the family vacation shoe basket and offered him his choice of footwear. Many options filled that basket, from sparkle to suede. Asher went through them carefully and finally chose the pink tennis shoes.

So, they weren't entirely pink. Almost orthopedic in style, the shoes were white leather with a pink zig-zag strap; Hello Kitty stared out from the side. Asher liked the Z-shaped closure. He liked the kitty.

My four-year-old boy, Asher, loved the shoes.

Full of males, our house has always tilted toward testosterone. Bodily functions are hilarious, and plastic weapons, accoutrement. Balls, trains, dinosaurs, and grossology we have studied to exhaustion. For a child well versed in all things "boy," and with an admired older brother as his life guide, Asher had made a choice that surprised me. When Truman was the same age, he had a strong aversion to anything "girl." He voiced his disgust of the color pink and with anything and anyone associated with it. Girls were the enemy. Girls and all their girlish props were girl-evil. Truman's job was to inform the masses about the girl scourge threatening them.

Afraid my feminist friends would discover I was harboring the enemy, I sought advice from anyone who allowed me to verbally process. My early-childhood-development guru-friend reassured me the sexist comments coming from Truman's lips were clearly a boy's way of figuring out his place in life. Just as good and evil collide in his imaginary warfare play, where his good guy always defeats the bad guy, this was the work of a boy navigating his world.

Despite what my guru and my gut told me, I was confused. A sexist? In my house?

Then the shoes showed up.

While my spouse's raised eyebrows said, "Uh, what?" I responded to the shoes with motherly support, spiced with a snicker. What an interesting research project, I thought, to observe Asher navigate through preschool life with blue jeans, a T. rex T-shirt, and those shoes.

When we got home from our beach vacation, Asher tossed his new shoes in the basket with the other pair he owns. Curious to know his continued feelings toward *the* shoes, I often suggested that pair when rushing to school in the morning. "What about *these* ones?"

Asher wore them several times over the next two weeks. He didn't mention if anyone commented on them at school, but I heard older neighbor kids frequently asking, "Why are you wearing girl shoes?" I was proud of him for being his own guy as he either ignored or internalized those comments. He liked the shoes.

Until he didn't.

I could tell Asher started contemplating his choice when he dressed for school each day. He wondered about the inevitable comments he would receive, and about whether assimilation might be easier. Asher's family supported him, quietly, but he heard society's message like a bullhorn. There was no confusion. Boys don't wear pink shoes.

Shoot. He gave in.

Often caught wallowing in the mud pit of mothering, I constantly second-guess my approach, or lack thereof, to parenting. Luckily for all of us, I am not the only parent in the house. While Brendon and I follow the traditional roles in our home—I cook and clean, he mows the lawn and tampers with the plumbing—I'm glad to have this man as my parenting partner. I will admit to spouting the cliché of "Wait until your father gets home" on a day when I'm most frazzled. While I hate when it comes out of my mouth, I really can't wait until he gets home.

Emerging as a happy accident in my life, one of Brendon's strengths has been his modeling and support of me in our home. He always invites our boys to love and respect Mom. They know where his heart is. There is no confusion.

"Who do we love?"

"Momma."

"Who do we take care of?"

"Momma."

While this teeters on the edge of "If mom ain't happy, ain't nobody happy," the message is clear: A partner is loved unconditionally and a mom is respected, even if she makes you and your pink shoes pick up the dog poop.

As a middle school teacher I witnessed confusion seep into every other moment of each kid's day. A girl once told me, "Henry keeps asking me if my underwear is blue." She was obviously upset. I talked to the boy. As I dug deeper into the conversation between the two, Henry admitted to asking the question.

I explained, "She was really bothered by it."

A confused look took over his face. "Really? But, she was laughing."

"Yeah, she was really uncomfortable, but felt as though she could only laugh about it. How do you think she felt talking about her underwear with you?"

Obviously misguided, he was confused; he didn't see her boundary. She was blind to it herself. She floundered between nervous laughter and an inappropriate situation, between commenting and saying nothing, between independence and assimilation. When he realized his line of questioning was not okay, his affect reflected a lesson learned.

Teachable moments occur daily for a mother. As I bumble through life with my boys, I take each potty-talking moment as it comes without much intentionality. But miracles do tousle my days. When I stop what I'm doing, grab the foam sword, and participate in the battle of knights. When I praise a positive rather than blast a negative—when I capture an unexpected hug. These small miracles affirm my parenting, telling me I might be doing something right.

Even on days when relentless sibling pestering seems without end, "No means no!" comes from my mouth like a love song. With my "no," I'm not only following through on my word, I'm clarifying the situation. No really does mean no. I've known too many girls whose "no" was not respected. It was ignored. Boundaries were crossed.

Mothering challenges my own boundaries, like when a pair of pink shoes shows up, a Hello-Kitty emblazoned miracle. Sometimes shoes are just shoes. Utility. Sometimes shoes are more purposeful than fancy footwear. This is not necessarily convenient, but neither is being a mother.

For a brief moment in time, my boys are young. They are fearless that way.

I love it.

All

Christin Taylor

Christin Taylor has a three-year-old daughter, Noelle. She lives in Bellingham, Washington, with her husband, Dwayne, where she runs The Blank Page writing workshops.

She earned her Master of Fine Arts in creative writing from Antioch University of Los Angeles. You can learn more about Christin and her writing at christintaylor.com.

I SIT PERCHED on the edge of Dar's leather chair while my two-year-old daughter clamors about my arms—her little palms gripping and pulling at my shirt. My mouth is half open, attempting speech, but nothing comes out. I imagine I look like a deer in headlights. Dar waits. I need an answer; I can't find one. My daughter, Noelle, howls, demanding my attention, and the moment speeds away from me. I follow Noelle's little blonde head over to the table for a drink, but Dar's words echo through my mind. "It's okay for women to lead in the secular realms, but in the church—no, that is a sin," she had said.

To meet someone who truly believes women are not spiritually equal to men took me thirty years. And even more remarkably, the person who seared my heart with this injustice is not in fact a man, but another mother whom I love deeply.

I met Dar a year-and-a-half ago, on a sunny morning while taking a walk with Noelle. We had recently moved to the desert of the San Gabriel Valley and were moseying along our new subdivision nestled up against the dry and crackling foothills. Noelle was eighteen months old and loved bumbling between the townhouses for mid-morning walks. On one of these mornings I followed her patiently across the grass and pavement, enjoying the sunshine and the sight of her little pudgy legs waddling back and forth. Noelle spotted a tricycle resting on a porch, and before I could stop her, she climbed on. Then the door of the house opened and a woman stepped out. She was petite, with black hair, and porcelain skin. Tucked in the crook of her arm was a tiny baby, just weeks old.

"Please, please," she said waving her free arm. "Please let her play. I have seen you walking before and meant to tell you that she can play with our toys." I detected an accent, but couldn't quite place it.

"My name is Dardana," she said, "but everyone calls me Dar. Please come in! Would you like some coffee?" She stepped aside, kicking some toys out of the way with her foot. Behind her I saw two more children playing in the living room: a boy who looked about three and a little girl about the same height as Noelle with soft, brown curly hair.

Immediately, I loved Dar because of her intelligent brown eyes and the thoughtful way she nodded when I spoke to her. I learned she was Albanian and had been raised under the Communist regime. She converted to Christianity during her high school years because of a group of Christian lawyers, and because of them, she also moved to America to study law and to work with children caught in human trafficking.

From that first morning on we met every week — basking in each other's presence, sharing stories, and enjoying motherhood together.

But on this particular morning, Dardana asks me, "Did you go to church this week?"

"Yes!" I say, excited to share with her our weekend. We had visited a Church of the Brethren congregation just a few blocks away from our apartment, and the experience was enlightening. "They had massive sunflower banners on either side of the pulpit," I tell her, "and the pastor wore a tie-dyed dress!" Dar's face suddenly contorts, and she shakes her head back and forth as if I have offered her garbage to eat.

I know Dar is feisty and carries that certain strain of Albanian determination, but I am stunned to see her react with such vehemence to my story. "Dar," I say, backtracking over our conversation. Noelle clamors onto my legs, pushing a book into my chest, "Mommy! Mommy! Read to me!"

"Dar," I repeat, taking the book from Noelle and pretending to read it. I am trying to buy more time. "Right then, when I talked about the female pastor, you made a face. Do you not believe in women in ministry?"

Without delay my friend responds. "No! That is not what God has intended! When women are over men in the church, all sorts of sin erupts. Oh no," she says again, shaking her head gravely. "It's not right."

I literally have no words. I have never before met anyone who truly believes it's a sin for women to be in ministry. She pauses for a moment and looks carefully into my eyes, "Why? Do you?" I hardly know where to begin to answer her.

Suddenly, I am embarrassed. My daughter Noelle is whining now. She places her fingers to her lips, signaling for a drink. I have no idea how to respond to Dar. I feel ashamed, as if somehow I believe heresy and have never recognized it as such. The words swallow up in my chest at that same spot where Dar's expression has lodged.

"Well," I stammer. "My grandmother was a pastor." Dar's brow crinkles. She looks genuinely worried. "On the mission field," I add, and then for some inexplicable reason, as if I feel I need to apologize, I say, "with my grandfather."

"Oh, well that is okay!" Dar throws her hands in the air with relief, as if she has pulled me back from a precipice. "If she was serving in conjunction with your grandfather, then that is okay. She would have been covered by him."

I walk away from this morning deeply shaken. And over the course of several days, my initial embarrassment wells up into confusion and then anger. I am not angry with Dar, but angry with myself for having thrown aside with such little care the heritage that has hung on my shoulders like so many rich cloaks.

The truth is, my paternal line glitters with female pastors.

I am the daughter of David, who is the son of Virginia, who is the daughter of Chloie. And there is no way to talk about my family tree without talking about the leafing out of the Wesleyan denomination beginning all those centuries ago with the sprout of the Pilgrim Holiness Church.

In 1895 my great-grandmother Meeks, Chloie, was born in Oblong, Illinois. In 1897 the Pilgrim Holiness Church was born in Cincinnati, Ohio. Chloie's parents were converted in a series of Pilgrim Holiness tent revivals, and she grew up in a church that from the very beginning ordained women. "They believed in the New Testament view of things," my grandmother explains to me over the phone. I've called her because all I remember of great-grandma Meeks is shrouded in the dimly lit sentimentality of memory. "The church believed that there is no male or female as far as God is concerned."

It was in the rich soils of this faith tradition that my great-grandmother's life took root. She became an ordained minister, a simple and profound step, and freedom coursed through the branches of her children's lives and her grandchildren's lives— that coursed all the way to me.

"She and my daddy pastored churches together up until I was in high school." In my mind's eye, I can see my grandmother's mouth. It is one of her most distinctive features because her smile is so wide. I inherited that smile: flat lips pulled across our gums to reveal the entire row of front teeth and two apple cheeks balled up beneath our eyes. Then there is her second most defining feature: the crown of cotton-white hair she inherited from her mother. I love hearing her talk about great-grandma Meeks. "Often Mother was the Sunday-morning preacher and Daddy handled the Sunday nights. They would switch back and forth. People always described it this way: Daddy was more evangelistic, and my mother was more nurturing. It was a wonderful combination."

I believe if you ask any one of my aunts, uncles, cousins, great aunts or uncles, they will tell you Chloie was the spiritual matriarch of our family, and that my grandmother, Virginia, has taken on her mantle with grace and ease.

"I've never felt called to preach," my grandmother continues. "My call was to missions and to teach, but I have been thrust into ministry from time to time." She is being modest. The truth is, she was trained to train pastors. She spent five years at Frankfort Bible School, in Frankfort, Indiana, earning her Bachelor in Theology degree, studying everything from church history to theology to missions.

When she met my grandfather, they moved to the Philippines to establish a Bible school. He managed the school and pastored the local church, while she taught Bible courses in addition to organizing Sunday school classes, which drew people from the community into the church.

Eventually my grandmother and grandfather moved to the capital, Manila, and found that the Wesleyan church there had no pastor—no one in the congregation willing to lead a big-city congregation. My grandfather's hands were full as the field superintendent, so the district superintendent asked my grandmother if she would be willing to pastor the church.

She prayed about it, thought about it, and then said, "Yes, if you will give me a Filipino graduate from the Bible school to help. Then I will take it." In this way, she was brought into the ministry and pastored that church for a handful of years while training up a gifted young Filipino named Abe Alejo to take her place.

So many decades later, I met Abe Alejo and witnessed the fruit of my grandparents' ministry. A large community of Filipinos from the Bible school had immigrated to California, planting Wesleyan churches in the cement and sun of Los Angeles. When my father turned fifty, the Alejos and three other families — whose lives were forever changed by the work my grandparents did in the Philippines — congregated at my parents' home to celebrate. They brought with them their children and their children's children, and covered the kitchen table with chicken adobo, pansit, and puto bumbong. There must have been nearly fifty people in my parents' home.

We sat in folding chairs in the backyard, the children playing in the grass around us. My grandmother and grandfather were directed toward the center, two chairs side by side. My grandparents beamed in the midst of all the bustle, the bodies flitting back and forth, Tagalog pattering out. My grandmother sat, her softly wrinkled hands folded carefully in her lap, her white hair lit by the sun, and that smile running across the years, on her face, my father's face, and my own. My grandmother's mouth has communicated so much truth over the decades.

A family friend once asked me, "Have you ever heard your grandmother preach?" I was living with my grandparents at the time, finishing my last semester of college while they were pastoring a small church in Mt. Etna, Indiana.

"No, I haven't," I admitted, and the absurdity of it struck me. How was this possible? That I had never actually heard her preach?

The family friend gawked in astonishment. "Oh, you *must*," he said. "She is a remarkable preacher."

It is with this heritage shaping my sense of spirituality and my sense of femininity that I run headlong into Dar's comments about women in ministry. And I wrestle with my inability to answer her—even while carrying the genes of these women pastors. Under the heat of Dar's gaze, why did I so quickly let that all go?

I think until that moment in her living room, I have revered Dar. Her testimony. Her motherhood. Her education. Here is a woman I admire, a woman from whom I am trying to learn, and suddenly, I see myself through her eyes: as someone who is either outside the realms of grace or so desperately misguided that she is nearly lost to salvation. The glimpse startles and frightens me.

Am I so misguided? Am I so fat on liberalism that somewhere, somehow, I have let go of the rich nourishment of truth?

I immediately go to my computer and e-mail the only people I can think of: my grandparents, my father, and my good friend Mandy, who is an ordained minister earning her Ph.D. from Princeton Seminary.

"It is not about man or woman," my grandfather reiterates. "It's about the work the Holy Spirit wants to do. And the Spirit is equally capable of using a woman to do his work as he is a man."

My friend Mandy adds, "I've studied long and hard about this, and I've finally come to believe that women are absolutely equal to men. In fact, I have a sort of righteous anger over churches who won't ordain women because I don't believe there is any way they can operate on all cylinders without allowing women in the ministry."

Besides giving me their overall opinions, they point me toward Bible verses and articles all defending the position of women in church. They name apostles who were women. "Look at the four daughters of Philip who were ordained," they say. "Or Deborah in the Old Testament."

But still Dar's crinkled brow and searching eyes pierce my heart.

One day my husband came home with a small blue book. The pages were yellow with years, and the thin cover was puckered and torn at the edges. Immediately, I recognized the name of the author: E. Stanley Jones. He was a famous missionary to India in 1908. During his time on the mission field he discovered a life-changing truth that would shape the future of missions across the Church. It was this: He could "preach Christ only; not Christ against a background of Western civilization." He went on to write fourteen books about his work in India, the most popular being *Christ of the Indian Road* and *Christ at the Round Table*.

Now, thinking about Dar, I seize Jones's book, flipping through the musty pages. In the contents I find these chapter titles:

"Mastery of special privilege and standing."

"Mastery of privilege based on blood."

"Mastery of social distinctions."

"Mastery of race distinctions."

"Mastery of the inferior status of women."

You can guess where I go first. I wish I could type for you all the words Jones writes about the injustice of the inferior status of women, but let me share simply the words that pierce my soul with Light:

At Pentecost 120 gathered together, including women, to pray. (Acts 1:14)

"And they were *all* filled with the Holy Spirit." (Acts 2:4 NKJV, emphasis added)

As Jones so beautifully articulates, that tiny word *all*, a word that can rest in the curl of your tongue and disappear from your mouth in a matter of seconds, includes the women with the men. The highest of heaven was open to women that day, and as Jones argues, why should not "the highest of earth be open to them as well?"

I hold Jones's book in my hands like a prayer, tears rolling down my face. "Dwayne!" I say, carrying my heart in the crease of the book, out to the living room where my husband lounges on the couch. "Listen to this." I begin to read.

> Alongside the almost universal practice of the subordi-
> nation of women to men, the Christians laid the in-
> compatible principle that women can and do receive
> the highest gift of God, the Holy Spirit: and it has
> silently worked against that evil practice and is in the
> process of overthrowing it.[1]

Dwayne smiles, and nods silently. In the other room, our own little girl lies sleeping, her protruding two-year-old belly lifting and falling, her pink lips curling around each breath.

She is Noelle, the daughter of Christin, the daughter of David, the son of Virginia, the daughter of Chloie. In her tiny body she carries the genes of women who have taught and led and pastored—who have lit the way for many souls around them. She is a little girl who will become a woman capable of receiving God's Holy Spirit and leading God's people, equal to any man in her life.

At the end of our conversation, my grandmother talks to me, woman to woman. She says, "If people will let us, God will use us where we are gifted. God has a way of doing that whether people like it or not." She laughs, and I imagine our smiles merging together across the miles, the same apple cheeks bunching beneath our eyes. "It happens. God thrusts us anyway—men or women—into places where we are needed and where we've been gifted to serve," then she stops and a new thought breaks in her head, "to get *God's* work done, not ours."

ENDNOTE

1. E. Stanley Jones, *Mastery: The Art of Mastering Life* (London: Hodder & Stoughton), 1956.

Precious in God's Sight

Jennifer Rouse

Jennifer Rouse is an award-winning newspaper reporter who used to spend her days writing about murder and mayhem for the *Albany Democrat-Herald*. She now writes mostly about her three daughters, whose antics are just as interesting but are far less likely to require daily trips to the county jail.

She; her husband, Eric; and their daughters, Beth (6), Lucy (4) and Evie (2) live in Oregon. You can keep up with her and "The Short Years" at jens_page.blogspot.com.

"MOM, there's a girl in my Sunday school class, but I don't know her name," Beth said to me.

I barely looked up from the socks I was sorting. "Well, what does she look like?" I asked.

"She's got black hair and brown skin and her eyes... ummm, her eyes are like this."

My head jerked up. Yep, my five-year-old was doing what I thought she was doing. With her fingers at the corners of her eyes, she was tugging the skin outward and upward, pulling her round brown eyes into a mockery of an Asian face.

My husband and I are like a lot of suburban white couples: We have three kids, we drive a minivan, we shop at Target. And we don't talk much about race.

Acknowledging somebody's race at all makes me feel awkward and vaguely guilty. Is it okay for me to bring it up? Should I say black or African American? Hispanic or Latino?

I grew up in a rural logging town in the Pacific Northwest; my husband is from an even smaller town in northern British Columbia. These places were not exactly brimming with diversity. We sang "Red and yellow, black and white; they are precious in his sight" at church, but we didn't actually interact with any of those other little children of the world whom Jesus supposedly loved. Just the white ones. (Nor did we realize, then, how offensive the song might be — that "yellow" in itself was a derogatory term for Asians.) When I did meet people of other races, I often worried that I might accidentally say something offensive. I did not purposely avoid people of other ethnicities, but my 90-percent-white geographic location and my own white-girl-insecurity kept my life nearly as segregated as a pre-Rosa-Parks-city bus.

But now, I find myself the mother of three pale-skinned blondes with sharp little minds that — like it or not — I am responsible for shaping. Racial attitudes and all.

It is pleasant to assume that my kids are naturally colorblind. In fact, many people willfully make this assumption — that if we don't ever draw attention to the way people look, our kids will grow up learning that physical differences are unimportant.

But pleasant as that idea might be, it's just plain wrong. Recent studies, such as one conducted at the University of Texas in 2006, have shown that kids naturally form their own ideas about race, often categorizing those who look like themselves as "nice" and those who look different as "mean."

And anyone who's been around kids very much can tell you that early psychologist Jean Piaget described them pretty well in the 1920s: miniature scientists, studying the world around them from the moment of birth. Children are constantly observing and categorizing. Mom's shirt is blue, just like my shirt! This rock is round, just like a ball! They're always thinking, always coming up with hypotheses to explain their observations. The thing is, young kids aren't very smart yet. A lot of their ideas are wrong.

When your baby tries to put a piece of dog food into her mouth because it's small, round, and looks like chocolate, you pull it out of her pudgy little fingers. She's made a wrong assumption. When your two-year-old thinks that because he can jump off the couch and land safely on his feet, he can also jump off the top of the jungle gym and land safely on his feet, you rush over and pull him down (or you wipe off his bloody knees after he hits the ground). He's made a wrong assumption.

When my daughter told me she didn't like being a girl because it meant she had to stay home and do all the work, I practically leaped to my feminist soapbox to explain to her that just because I am a stay-at-home mom does not mean she has to become one. I reminded her that while I may not go away to work in an office like daddy, I do get paid for the work I do as a freelance writer. I reminded her of her aunt and her grandmother who both hold full-time paying jobs. I all but ordered her to dream big dreams and be whatever she wanted to be when she grew up. She had made a wrong assumption about gender, and I rushed to correct it.

Why, then, do I find myself reluctant to talk about race with my children? Why don't these discussions come as naturally to me? Maybe it's my own lack of experience, the fear that I'll mess up on this important topic — the awkward feeling that whatever words come out of my mouth sound forced and cheesy, like I'm repeating the words of an after-school special rather than passing on important truths about life.

After all, my girls are getting a more diverse upbringing than I had. There are a handful of African-American students at my daughter's elementary school. We go to a church that is made up of a mix of many different races. My girls get to play with kids whose chocolaty skin and curly hair look different from their own. That's enough, right?

No. It's not. Not really. And I knew that as I watched my daughter innocently contort her face in an effort to describe another child's appearance. Kids need tools. They need the words to describe the differences that are clearly visible in the people around them; it's my job as a parent to provide that.

So I stopped folding laundry and sat down on the couch beside my five-year-old.

"Sweetie, do you mean the girl in your Sunday school class has eyes shaped differently than yours? Maybe kind of slanted?"

"Yes! That's how her eyes are," Beth said, still pushing hers upward.

"Well, I don't know her name, but it sounds like she's probably Asian," I said. "And you shouldn't pull on your eyes to make them look like that, because people might think you're making fun of her."

"I wasn't making fun," Beth was genuinely dismayed. "I was just showing you how her eyes look."

"I know, kiddo. But some white people used to treat Asian people badly. They liked to make fun of Asians because their faces look different from ours, and they would do it by slanting their eyes up like that."

"Oh." She sat quietly for a moment before piping up with a new question. "Mom, what's Asian?"

And so we talked for a few minutes, about geography and history, China and Japan and Vietnam, and that fact that in our country, people from all different parts of the world can come here and look different and have a different family history and still be American.

Then she ran off to play. We had a conversation about race, and it really wasn't a big deal.

I'm seeking them out now—little moments like that. Chances to comment upon someone's race rather than turn away from it: when President Obama is on the cover of a magazine; when we read *Little House on the Prairie* and the characters talk about how the "Indians" will have to leave their land because white settlers are moving in; and when we hear a family at the grocery store speaking Spanish to one another. We can teach our children about the vast variety of God's creation. We can admire its complexity and call it good.

Yesterday Beth caught my attention again. "I'm going to make this very hard to believe," she said, studying the picture she was about to color. It was a Valentine's Day picture, showing a man and a woman, hand in hand, a heart over their heads. Beth looked at the cartoonish couple and said, "I'm going to make her a white and him a black!"

And oh, I cringed over the awkward words she used. I cringed over her idea that a biracial couple was "hard to believe." But I loved what she was trying to express.

"Well, sweetie, it's true that we don't know many couples where the people are each of different races. But there are couples like that, and just because you don't know many of them doesn't mean it's hard to believe," I said.

And she finished, filling in my words before I had a chance to. "Because we can love anybody, no matter what color they are," she said with a grin. And then she pulled out her darkest brown crayon and began to color.

Uniquely Qualified

Marilee Jolin

Marilee Jolin is mommy to Mira (3) and Melina (1). While her daughters are young, Marilee is keeping her non-mommy aspirations alive through her blog (thecontemplativemommy.com) and other writing pursuits, while working toward her ultimate goal of peace and mediation work overseas.

She is currently living in western Washington.

AT MY daughter Mira's two-year "well child" checkup, the doctor, going down the list of developmental milestones, asked if my daughter knew the difference between boys and girls. I smiled. Rather than sharing any of Mira's more colorful comments as she watches me breastfeeding her new sister or sees her dad exit the shower, I simply answered that yes, she does know the difference.

What I didn't tell the doctor is that I constantly worry that Mira's knowledge of the difference between boys and girls is not the understanding I would like her to have. As her prime example of womanhood, I sometimes fear I am a poor model of independence and strength.

My journey toward my Ph.D. ended when Mira was born. I know putting school on hold was the right choice, and I'm glad to be able to stay home with her. Still, I sometimes feel my daily activities of diapers, dishes, laundry, and play dough do not give Mira the clear message I'd like to send her about female ability and ambition. I realize we are fortunate to be able to get by on one income, and that many women would be thrilled to quit their jobs and stay home with their kids. But for me it feels like a failing of sorts.

I often think many of my friends are better role models for my daughter. The friend on a trip around the world; the friend graduating from medical school; the friend serving as a social worker in the inner city; or the friend teaching school in Indonesia: They all exhibit levels of empowerment and independence in their daily actions that I can only illustrate with words. I've heard it many times: Your words only go so far. Children are most influenced by what you do. You can prattle all you want about following your dreams and not conforming to the norm; what your daughter will remember is you cooking dinner every night, waiting for her father to return home with the bacon.

It's like a story my sister told me about her oldest daughter, Elaina, who was about eight at the time. Elaina's teacher tried to help her brainstorm ways to decorate a Mother's Day card by asking what her mother liked best to do. Elaina thought for a long time, and then finally responded: "Well, I guess she likes to clean. And cook." I laughed when my sister told me this story, but there was an edge to my laughter: Had my intelligent, competent sister who put her counseling career on hold to raise her kids really been reduced to this? In reality, there is much more to her life than cooking and cleaning, but it bothered me that this was all that had made an impression on eight-year-old Elaina.

I desperately want my daughter to see that I am capable of everything and to therefore know that *she* is capable of everything—able to tackle every challenge thrown at her and qualified for any career, any path she can imagine. And I am constantly afraid she will grow up seeing only a mother who cooks and cleans. I have a long list of aspirations and goals that are in no way forgotten; they are simply "on hold." But how do I ensure that those dreams are not swallowed up and lost in the rush of kids getting older?

Last Christmas we got a new book about a family preparing for the holidays. When we reached the page about baking Christmas cookies I beamed. *Way to go author,* I thought, pleased to see the fictional father cooking with the kids while the mother sits at the computer.

"Look, Mira," I said happily. "The daddy is baking cookies."

Mira scrunched up her nose and furrowed her eyebrows. "No," she said, laughing. "Daddies don't cook!"

I was crushed. Really? *Really?* At eighteen months old she's saying this? She seemed to be merrily skipping down the path to prescribed gender roles: My mommy likes to cook and clean!

I realize, of course, that I am overreacting. She is so young. Developmentally, her understanding of gender roles has barely progressed beyond biological differences. At this point it's pretty much about who has "boobies" and who does not. As I breastfeed her infant sister she likes to regale me with the list of who has this defining female feature (Mommy does; Grandma does; Daddy doesn't). But still, because these early years build a foundation, I want Mira's to be a foundation of equality. I want her to know men and women are equals, equally loved by God, equally able to do all things.

So I do what I can. I constantly read my two girls the book about the female Emperor Penguins going off to hunt while the male penguins hatch the eggs. We call my periodic writing trips to the coffee shop "work," and I love to hear my husband say as the door closes behind me: "Daddy went to work this morning, now it's Mommy's turn to go to work." I make a concerted effort to not over-compliment my daughters' looks but to equally praise their intelligence, toughness, and sense of humor. I try to keep sports equipment and a reasonable number of trucks in Mira's toy box to balance out her love of dolls and kitchens.

And has it made a difference? I really don't know how to tell. Mira no longer laughs at the book with the dad baking cookies, and she doesn't bat an eye when Mommy goes to work. She hasn't yet asked me where God belongs on her booby list, and I'm chocking that up as a win for egalitarianism. I'm sure someday she will want to assign God a gender, and she may ask me if girls are as strong as boys. (Or as smart, God forbid.) And I guess I'll just have to handle those conversations when they come.

For now, it's all about loving her, talking to her, and being myself. And trusting that even without the Ph.D., the trip around the world, or the established career, I am Mira's mother, and I care more than anyone that she will grow up to be an empowered woman. And, of course, that makes me uniquely qualified to teach her exactly what she needs to know.

Digging for Answers

Emily Chadwick

Emily Chadwick is the personal chef, laundress, chauffer, and story reader extraordinaire for Nolan (4) and Laurel (3). She writes a newspaper column, "On a Shoestring," in which she examines living on a budget while embracing the notion that less is more.

She's learning to be content with her backyard garden in Carlton, Oregon, with hopes of someday living on a bit more earth.

"STINKING FLIES." Thwack. The man's quick spatula maneuver saved the stack of flapjacks near the Coleman stove. "Disgusting," he murmured and flipped another cake on the griddle. As he took a swig from the blue enameled coffee mug and kicked a bottle of bug repellent under the picnic table, a mess of fleece and stocking cap pushed aside the tent flap. Rubbing sleep from his eyes, a young child stumbled out, ready for breakfast. The father stopped cooking to drop a dollop of pink calamine on the boy's cheek, soothing the itch of a swollen mosquito bite. Meanwhile, a fly landed near a plate of bacon. Thwack.

When camping on the Oregon Coast, warm evenings give way to foggy, wet mornings just as sure as pesky bloodsuckers around the campfire become garbage flies at the breakfast table. The image of a father taking life one minute and sweetly tending to the needs of his child the next caused me little reason to pause when I was twenty—nearly a decade before I became a mother. The image washed over me and into the water lapping the shoreline a short distance away. But a single drop of water is never actually lost, and the memory of witnessing this came full circle all these years later.

I've never been one to think twice about flushing a spider found crawling on the bathroom floor. I've squished countless bugs with no reason beyond dislike of creepy-crawlies. And in college, like many youth on the brink of self-discovery, I played exterminator one minute and "saved animals" as a vegetarian the next. I tried on existentialism like a coat off the department store rack. Experience without real personal investment is like that sometimes. Motherhood, however, woke me up to a sense of convictions oceans beyond the passing phases of my youth. Everything matters when you're renamed "Mama," even thwacking flies.

*   *   *

"When I finally land that country home, I'll plant an herb garden." It was the fourth time in a week this spilled from my mouth. We have no immediate plans to move, though we'd love to. It could happen in a few months or five years from now. Life sometimes complicates dreams, but I keep my eye on the future — nearly to a fault. I'm a planner, which is good. But I plan and plan and plan, always looking for the right time or place to tackle whatever it is that I've been dreaming about doing. My ideal plan was to move and then start an herb garden. The thing is, my present yard is already the perfect place for growing a thing or two.

In recent years I have embraced the truth that sometimes the right time is simply the moment we risk a spontaneous jump to live outside of a carefully calculated plan. The right time is the moment we decide to make it so. Thinking about this, I jumped headfirst, gathered the children, and planted an herb garden.

I hold a strong belief that my children will learn the courage to live their dreams when they see me doing the same. I certainly fall short at times, but on my best days I live with intention and move toward my goals. While planting an herb garden isn't exactly on par with a book deal or ending world hunger, it nonetheless was something I both wanted and put off while I searched for greener pastures.

The decision to move forward, no matter how big or small the undertaking, always fills me with a giddy lightness. The day after I decided to plant the garden, I nearly floated on my way to my son's preschool. As I made my way to the play yard to pick up my son, I felt light, even though my thirty-five pound toddler rested on my hip. After a morning of rain, my daughter and I welcomed the warm sunshine as we walked, and we lingered more than usual as we made our way down the path. Inner peace does this. It opens the door for lingering, for laughing, for noticing.

The teacher saw me and then called my son. While Nolan took part in the shaking-hands formality and said his good-byes, I noticed a patch of dirt on the side of the school. But upon closer examination, I saw not dirt, but spider's eggs. They were hatching. Hundreds of tiny spiders were emerging into chaos, scrambling to make sense of new life, to make sense of this world they'd landed in. As I pointed out this miracle to my children, I was struck: What a short time ago it was that my own babies entered this world. The loving arms that welcomed them were a sharp contrast to this birth, their mother long gone, as is the way in the lifecycle of a spider.

"Do you suppose Charlotte's in there?" I asked my children. They shook their heads to indicate no.

Then very seriously my son asked, "Mommy, who will take care of all the babies?"

Had we discovered these spider eggs inside my house, my reaction would have likely been different. I have no desire to see spiders all over my walls, and surely I would have found my own way to "take care" of them. But here in the outdoors, observing the beginning of life, even spiders filled me with wonder and reverence.

"Life is a precious gift," I said to my son, surprised to find just the right words when I needed them. As we walked into the school building to grab his coat, I continued, "Don't worry about the babies; there is a plan for them. Spiders have important work to do in this world."

We were nearly out the door when we ran into another teacher.

"We saw spiders hatching!" Nolan said, excited to share his news. This led to the teacher sharing a story about an unexpected caterpillar hatch and infestation in the school last year. Nolan seemed interested and told her that insects are important.

"Except for beetles," he said with the authority of one who knows much about bugs and life. "We have to squish those."

Like in most of my awkward oops-we-need-to-work-on-that parenting moments, I made a quick exit and wondered how one goes about teaching respect for all life in a society that seems so programmed to take life without thought.

*   *   *

"They're just beetles, right?" I repeated silently to myself all the way home, knowing my actions were the source of his comment. Since the first spring rains, our garage had been full of beetles, and until that moment in the school, I hadn't thought twice about squishing them. How can a young child understand a hierarchy as complicated as human over beast, and some beasts over other beasts, and that some life we consider so insignificant that we squash it with a shoe or slather the ground with dangerous chemicals to wipe it out and we never think twice? How can I understand it? And never mind the fact that this is *not* the attitude I mean to impart on my children, but nevertheless, this *is* the message I sent when I tried to keep the insects from infesting my home and didn't explain my actions to the kids. It's moments like these that manuals for raising respectful, loving, compassionate, and thoughtful citizens would be handy.

Without a manual, I did what I could. "Help me with this one," I prayed, and then gathered up the tools for grass removal. I didn't have a plan to deal with complicated philosophical elucidations and ideological debates with my preschooler, but I did have a plan to dig a garden plot.

Sometimes you find what you need in the last place you look. The garden spade was my fourth pick as I systematically failed to effectively move sod with every other tool my husband had stocked in the shed. But one jab at the roots with the spade, and we were able to peel large chunks of sod right off the ground.

"Oh, a worm!" my daughter shouted as we tore back the first piece.

"Actually, that's a larva," I said, and gave a simple explanation of metamorphosis.

The more sod we peeled back, the more larvae we found. Suddenly I understood why my lawn looked the fright it did; unbeknownst to me, I'd been playing hostess to an endless backyard bug buffet. They were everywhere under the grass, a sign that the natural systems in our yard were out of balance, which somehow seemed fitting given the rest of the chaos in our lives: discontentment with our living situation and the challenges that come with two young children in the house.

"Mommy, the larvae are kind of like the baby spiders," said Nolan while his sister searched for earthworms. I was surprised how much of my earlier explanation about the stages of insect life he had absorbed. Then when my daughter decided to trade her night-crawler hunt for larvae stomping, Nolan stopped her.

"Laurel, these are babies. We don't want to squish them. Gently put them in the wagon with the grass and dirt."

As we continued removing sod, Nolan kept instructing his sister to put each newly uncovered larva into the wagon with its "brothers and sisters." We worked for a long time. I wondered if I should tell the children that the larvae were not exactly welcome guests in our yard, that there is a chemical we could put on the grass to get rid of them. I chose not to mention it.

"Are hunters bad?" Nolan suddenly asked. I could tell he'd been chewing on the question for a while.

"I guess it depends on who you ask," I said. "People have been hunting and gathering food for a very long time."

"Hunters kill, right?"

"Yes."

"And killing is bad, right?"

I wasn't prepared for this conversation. Earlier in the day my son took delight in telling his teacher he smashed beetles. A few hours and an herb garden later, and now he was asking big questions about life and death.

"We are all part of an ecosystem, Nolan, where one life supports another. Animals hunt for food," I said.

"Like a coyote hunts a mouse?" he asked.

"That's right. The coyote eats the mouse. The mouse isn't alive anymore. The coyote must do that to live," I explained.

He seemed to understand. It's difficult to know what to say to a young child. I didn't want to frighten him, but I try to give my children information that is both honest and appropriate.

"When people hunt," I explained, "They too are looking for food to help them live. Some things die so that others don't die, but the decision to end life is a serious one. Life is a precious gift; the decision to end it should never be taken lightly."

"Even beetles, Mommy?" he said.

"Even beetles," I said, and then my thoughts circled back to the camper swatting flies a lifetime ago at the Oregon Coast. I understand far better now the places parenthood pushes us. Sometimes it's keeping our children's food clean by chasing away the flies. Other times, it is learning to live with whatever lies beneath the grass.

Knowing the True Light

Art thou a child of Light and has walked in the Light,
and what thou speakest is it inwardly from God?

(George Fox)

Guilty: A Church-Skipping Mom

Ellen Painter Dollar

Ellen Painter Dollar is a writer and mother living in West Hartford, Connecticut. She has written about faith, motherhood, and disability for *Christianity Today*, the American Medical Association, the Osteogenesis Imperfecta (OI) Foundation, the *Hartford Courant*, and the Episcopal Café. She blogs at "Choices That Matter" (choicesthatmatter.blogspot.com), focusing on reproductive ethics; and "Five Dollars and Some Common Sense" (thefivedollars.blogspot.com), where she writes about everything else, especially life with three children, a chronic bone disorder, and a Christian faith that is not easily pigeonholed.

SEVERAL SUNDAYS ago my kids were playing outside when we called them to get in the car for church. They stalled. They whined. They asked, "Why do we always have to go to church?" My responses became less patient and my words sharper, until I slammed my hand against the steering wheel and said through clenched teeth, "Going to church is *what we do*. Get used to it."

We all arrived at church grumpy—an unfortunately common state on Sunday mornings. The following Sunday, we used the fact that it was "Youth Recognition Sunday" (often a particularly long, dull service) as an excuse to skip church. And now that it's summer, we, like many families, will probably find more excuses over the next two months to not attend. We'll be away some weekends, and we relish breaks from getting everyone up and out the door by a specific time. Judging by the sparsely occupied pews in many churches during this season, we aren't the only family who skips church more often in the summer.

A few years ago, such a lax attitude toward church attendance was unthinkable to me. We were die-hard churchgoers, in the pews every Sunday barring illness or vacation. But being a die-hard means you are given jobs, and when you do those jobs well, you are given more jobs. Sunday worship ceased to be a time of renewal; it was work. When we joined our current parish two years ago, I was determined to be more deliberate and cautious about volunteering. Being less involved makes Sunday mornings more enjoyable, but having fewer responsibilities also makes it easier to skip Sunday services altogether.

Our kids are thrilled when we take a Sunday off. But our newly relaxed attitude toward church attendance raises important questions: Are we modeling a nebulous spirituality, teaching our kids to pick and choose from among religious practices while rejecting anything that requires real commitment? Is it possible to engage in life-giving, sacrificial commitment without falling into energy-draining, resentment-breeding burnout? Perhaps most important: How do I instill faith in my children, and how important is church attendance in that endeavor?

A living faith requires both communal obligations and private disciplines. We as a family pray before dinner, read Bible stories, and teach the religious meaning of major holidays with traditions such as Advent candles and Lenten mite boxes. When one of my kids is struggling with disappointment or fear, I offer prayer as the best action when you don't know what else to do.

Is this enough for their budding faith? Can it withstand occasional Sunday mornings away from church? Can we dig in the garden or read a good book instead?

I'm not sure. My own faith journey has been unpredictable. I grew up in the Episcopal church, the daughter of a talented and supremely likable Episcopal clergyman. I am an Episcopalian again, but only after years of trying other styles of worship—an evangelical college fellowship, an urban coffeehouse church. Although my father has influenced me, my faith journey has been my own, just as my kids' faith journeys must be their own. I can provide a foundation, but I cannot control which people, places, or experiences will most influence their eventual embracing or rejecting of faith.

I want to give my children all the things experts say make children resilient and happy, then sit back knowing they will be all right. Such assurance is impossible. A few weeks ago, I was immersed in reading *Beautiful Boy*, David Sheff's haunting memoir about his son's meth addiction, as my children played outside with the neighbors. As I read and listened to the kids' joyful noise, I thought, "It's not enough. None of these benefits—unstructured outdoor play, caring parents, safe and friendly neighborhood—are certain to protect them from addiction, illness, betrayal, despair, or failure." I want faith, along with family dinners, reliable routines, healthy friendships, and loving parental supervision, to inoculate my children against all that would harm them and all the ways they can harm themselves. But there is no such vaccine.

I can only hope that our faith and practice—including making church an integral part of our life, but also embracing occasional Sundays spent at home—will help our kids reach toward the Light, trusting it is there even when they are swallowed up in darkness. And I do strive to hold Sundays up as a different sort of day even when we do not go to church. My personal discipline of honoring the Sabbath means engaging in no writing work, refraining from computer usage other than a quick e-mail check now and then, and only doing chores that we can participate in as a family, such as gardening. We spend most Sundays at home, together.

The other night, my daughter approached me and asked, "Do you have to pray to God out loud, or does God hear your prayers if they are silent?" I assured her that silence was just fine. I don't know what she was praying about, though I have my suspicions. But this—a desire to connect with God—is really what I want for my kids. I want faith to be what we do, a way of living and seeing the world that buttresses our life together, even if we take a summer Sunday off from church now and then.

Superhero Jesus

Rebekah D. Schneiter

Rebekah Schneiter is the mother of three boys, Bren (6), Coen (4), and Aren (2). Her boys have many adventures on their farm outside of Eugene, Oregon.

Readers in Newberg, Oregon, have followed her parenting trials and tribulations through her column, which regularly appears in *The Newberg Graphic.* Her work has also appeared in MOPS (Mothers of Preschoolers) International publications and is part of the "What You Wish You Would Have Said" project.

Without guilt she serves her boys mac and cheese from a box and pacifies them with fruit snacks in the van. You can read more about her outnumbered life at rebekah-outnumbered.blogspot.com.

I THINK I've created a superhero Jesus, complete with cape, tights, and death-defying powers.

This kind of Jesus became necessary after we made a major move from the "city" back to the farm, to the very house I grew up in. The transition proved hard on my oldest son, Bren; even the little things seemed rough on him. Bren went from sharing a small room with his little brother Coen, to having a huge room all by himself—a room that is upstairs while his dad and I are downstairs. Here in the great nowhere, nights actually get completely dark. And even though we are able to see the stars now, these stars hardly comfort a scared little boy with an active imagination.

The night's shadows seem extra creepy in a farmhouse bedroom — especially this bedroom. I should know; I slept in it as a child and am familiar with its scary monsters, creaks in the floorboards, and groans as it shifts in the night. These sounds are real. And to Bren, they are the sounds of things that want to hurt and attack him, mean and scary. I gladly leave the hallway light on for Bren until he falls asleep. I hated it when my own mom would turn the same hallway light off, and tell me that if I said the name of Jesus all the scary creatures would run away. I held very tightly to this idea and would fall asleep chanting the name "Jesus." I hardly allowed myself breath between utterances.

Jesus was my garlic necklace.

Remembering the fears I had, I didn't want my little boy to be as afraid as I was growing up in that bedroom, controlled by scary thoughts. I wanted him to know Jesus was with him, loving and taking care of him. Jesus was there even when mommy and daddy weren't. He could talk to Jesus. Listen to Jesus. Experience Jesus. I have big plans for my child's spirituality. That is why I eagerly announced, "Jesus is with you, Bren. He is keeping you safe."

"Where is he?"

Good question. I was dumbfounded. Is this when I talk about Jesus being the Light within us? All of a sudden this very comforting idea of Christ being the Light, seeking relationship with all creation, seemed potentially a little scary, too, so I fumbled and reverted to an old childhood metaphor: "Well, Jesus lives in our hearts — when we ask him to."

I was conflicted: I wanted my child to know Jesus was already in a loving relationship with him, but I also want my child to have a "moment" when he asks Jesus to be his redeemer, friend, Savior, ever-present Lord, and Messiah: all the important "Christianese" stuff that reassures those who ask about when you became a Christian. This prayer, often repeat-after-me, gives you a date to write down in your journal so you can remember when you made that fateful decision. Like a security blanket.

My son seemed a bit young to get the whole sin-forgiveness concept, however. Wasn't the main idea to make him aware of Christ holding and loving him, keeping him safe? So I decided to emphasize the safe part. He wanted to say a little prayer, to get the deed done. The prayer went something like, "Jesus, live in my heart and keep the monsters away."

Since then Jesus has done some heroic things in Bren's life. At night Christ jumps out of my son's heart and becomes big. Normally Jesus is really small, since he has to fit into our hearts, but at night his superhero abilities kick in and he's able to fight off all the monsters with a "wappy" thing.

Jesus also makes all sorts of cool creations: sunsets, moun-tains, tractors, bridges, and various toys. When I tried to ex-plain that God made people, and God helped those people understand how to make the bridges, Bren looked at me like I was crazy, "No mommy, God made them," he said. This was his God, his superhero Jesus. Why wouldn't he fly down and build that bridge?

Bren has begun to teach these finer points of doctrine to his younger brother. I hear Bren lecturing on how Jesus is in our hearts and how God makes us and cars and trucks—all the important things. My youngest just smiles and announces, "I'm a lion," and then roars impressively.

I mentioned my concern to a friend. "I think I've created a superhero Jesus for my son."

"That's kind of a nice idea, saving you and all. I like that," she said. She made a very appropriate superhero sound and did some cool thing with her arms so that she looked like a muscular being flying through the air. I laughed.

I'm not sure what I thought as a young girl when I asked Jesus into my heart. Did I think a little man resided there? Did I wonder how he fit? All I remember was wanting Jesus. It felt right. It felt safe. I had read a book about a little boy who tried to be good, but often wasn't. I related completely. I asked my mom if I could pray like the little boy and ask Jesus to live in me. I was elated that night. I remember strumming my Smurf guitar and singing self-written songs. And I talked Jesus' ear off. I told him everything. My mom had said I could. I'm sure I told Jesus all about my dolls, my sister, my adventures outside, and everything that matter to a five-year-old.

Now my son is sharing those ideas that matter to him, and God is listening. They are in relationship. Jesus is real to my son. Bren talks to Jesus like you would to a friend or relative. Except you can't see Jesus, and Bren is working through this.

When Bren announced that Jesus can't talk back to him, I told Bren that Christ can and is speaking, but Bren just needs to listen. (As if I have this totally down myself—listening and hearing God.) The next morning Bren told me he *can* in fact talk to Jesus, and that Jesus talks back. Even though Bren might not fully grasp God's existence, he doesn't doubt it; he relies on it. (Do any of us ever fully get God?) Bren loves Jesus, and Jesus loves Bren. Jesus keeps Bren safe. Who knows, maybe at night Jesus really does become huge and hurl monsters off Bren's bed.

I don't think I have completely ruined my son's spirituality. I hope I've actually jump-started his awareness of a loving God, even if God currently wears tights and a cape and carries a "wappy" thing.

Knowing Place

Lee Snyder

Lee Snyder, president emeritus of Bluffton University, is active in denominational and leadership activities as well as writing. Her book, *At Powerline and Diamond Hill: Unexpected Intersections of Life and Work*, was published in 2010.

In retirement, Lee and her husband, Del, divide their time between Virginia and Oregon. They enjoy travel and spending time with their families, including two daughters and four grandchildren. And with a passion for literature, Lee always has a stack of books to read in between walking and watching movies.

"WHY would you want to do this?"

I was startled by the question. Although it was an unseasonably cold Ohio night in early November 1995, it had not occurred to me to bring a winter coat. My husband and I found our way to the designated lounge, waiting to be summoned for a reception at which I would be introduced as the presidential candidate for Bluffton College. "Why would you want to do this?"

It was a good question, one which at the time I could not have answered adequately. This stately, elegant trustee wife, who also was waiting for the trustees to finish their session and for the candidate reception to follow, was gracious but direct. She sized me up, wondering why a woman would want such a job. Or more to the point, what audacity had brought me to Bluffton? I do not remember what I said; I must have stammered, searching for the polite response. How much did I reveal about my own uncertainties? For the truth is I was not sure I did want the job.

But this is getting ahead of the story, which starts with a place and the year a five-year-old meets God personally. For one growing up in the 1940s and early 1950s on an Oregon ryegrass farm in a close-knit Mennonite community, God was the main thing. Even before being aware of myself, really, I had developed a private and personal sense of God as the center of the universe—not only in the prescribed rituals of church and home but through the raw splendor of a life dependent on planting and harvest, on rain and sun, on dirt and fertility.

It was a place of abundance, but also of tragic losses. I cannot remember when I first learned that I had been named after my father's seven-year-old sister who died of diphtheria. I knew the names of my twin brothers almost as soon as I knew my own name. To a two-year-old, Donald and Ronald were there but not there. My mother's private grieving for these babies born too soon was revealed only by a recitation, when I would ask, of just the bare facts: Donald lived two-and-a-half hours, and Ronald lived three. Over the years, when I would return to the Willamette Valley to visit my parents, the short story of my twin brothers' lives was extended by afternoon or evening walks down to the Alford Cemetery, where my mother and I visited the simple gravestones there in the shadow of the tall cedar next to the great-grandparents.

Where God was in all this—and in my teenage cousin's accident that occurred while helping his grandfather with the harvest—was not clear. When he got his legs caught in the combine auger, we could not bear to imagine those amputated limbs. But, in general, circumstances were — well — just what they were.

Loss was cushioned by an unshakable and unquestioning faith, structuring daily routines. Our lives were ordered by nightly Scripture reading, while prayer at mealtimes dispensed a thrice-daily dose of gratitude. To ravenous children, these prayers were interminably long. And they seemed purposely extended when the telephone happened to ring while our heads were bowed and my father refused to be hurried. For us kids sitting around that chrome table in the dining room, we waited to see which would happen first — the caller giving up, or Dad ending his prayer in time for one of us to make the mad dash to the phone before it stopped ringing.

But meeting God personally was another matter. Looking back, there is the indelibly etched image of a particular day, and a child weighed down by the intensity of a private encounter. Is this a real memory or a collage of images that have taken on a life of their own? Walking home from school, head bent into the wind, shivering in a thin blue coat, the child is hardly aware of the dead sky or the pelting sleet as she prays. As she treks down the road toward the farmhouse, the dormant fields are folded into the awful silence. Even the girl's shoes make no sounds against the wet gravel of the pavement. With a child's unmitigated belief, absorbed from the life of the church community, this girl knows God is real and that God means what God says.

My first crisis of faith, I now realize — and a marker along the way toward discovering my place in the God-scheme — came when I was six. I lost my most prized possession: a maroon Gideon New Testament. I was devastated. When it did not turn up after much searching, I began praying that God would give it back. My prayers became pleading, demanding, "Please, God. Please, God."

How many days did these relentless prayers go on? Did my mother become concerned when I asked four, five, or six times a day where else we could look? I imagine Dad obliging me when I thought of yet another place to check, down behind the seat cushions of the Chevy.

Even after Mom and Dad had exhausted every possibility in helping me search for the New Testament, I hung on to a grim hope that my prayer would be answered. Going to bed, buried in one of the family quilts, I tried to think of ways God might respond. I knew that God, so choosing, could simply open up the heavens, reach down, and return the New Testament. It was as simple as that. There was the story from Sunday school where God meets Moses but allows Moses only to see God's back. Maybe I would be allowed to see God's hand reaching down out of the clouds, handing me the Testament?

My prayers continued for days, with a fierce insistence and unwavering belief that God would intervene and honor the promise, "Ask and you shall receive." While my parents knew how much I wanted my Bible back, I have no idea if they sensed the desperate drama going on between their oldest child and God. What would heaven do with a six-year-old who believed that God was going to literally give back the Testament?

God gave it back.

While the details remain hazy, it must have happened something like this: One evening a car pulled up into the driveway. A man got out and knocked on the door. From way on the other side of town, Mr. Edwards showed up at the door. "I brought something I think your little girl must have left at our place the other week when you stopped in," he said. "We found this after you left." In his had, Mr. Edwards held out the maroon Testament. "I was just driving over this way anyway, and my wife thought your daughter might want this back."

I did not even hear my father thank Mr. Edwards. It was not until Dad had closed the front door that I could move.

"Here you are," Dad said. "I knew it would turn up."

Mom, hearing the commotion, came in from the kitchen, drying her hands on her apron. "Where did that come from?" she asked, looking first at Dad, then at me.

"Mr. Edwards dropped it off. We left it at their house when we went over to see their house plans."

All Mom said was, "I had no idea you took your Bible along."

She went back to clean up the kitchen. Dad took up his reading. The household settled back to normal.

While that experience appears to an adult as embarrassingly naïve, I have no doubt that God answered my prayer. It was as though the heavens had opened and God had handed back my Testament.

That child-God encounter was one marker along the way of discovering one's place—a place in the God-scheme of things. Finding one's place, both literally and figuratively, reaches toward the ineffable and yields glimpses of both the imagined and the not-yet-in-our-consciousness. That place is where we start.

One Small Miracle

Bolivia, 1980

Nancy J. Thomas

Nancy Thomas, poet and missionary, has spent her life in cross-cultural ministry in Latin America. Married to Hal, she is mother to David and Kristin, mother-in-law to Debby and Jon, and grandma to seven.

She has the vocation of training Latin American Christian writers, and is the author of several publications, which include *The Secret Colors of God* (Barclay Press, 2005). Nancy's blog, "Mil gracias," is at nancyjthomas.blogspot.com.

BALOFUR'S TIMING was perfect. Our slight black cat, bewildered and inexperienced, began giving birth to her first litter just as the kids got home from school. Fascinated, we all sat on the rug to watch and encourage.

Our fascination quickly changed to concern as Balofur struggled with the second kitten. She groaned and strained, rested awhile, and tried again, seemingly in vain. Accusation and confusion mingled in the look she threw me, and somehow I felt personally responsible. The kids were worried, and I certainly didn't know what to do. Finally in desperation I turned cat midwife, gently pulling until kitten number two slid out. Balofur then easily gave birth to the third and last kitten.

The first and third kittens soon began whining and searching for sustenance. Nature seemed to have the situation well in hand. The still-confused mother tentatively pawed and licked, beginning to understand that these ragged pieces of fur belonged to her.

But kitten number two was a pathetic sight. Not a sound found its way from his throat. Not a single movement of spindly limbs groped toward warmth or food. He just lay there, and every few seconds gasped for air, followed by a brief sharp convulsion. Somewhat objectively, keeping pity at an adult minimum, I observed to myself, "This cat is not going to make it."

But David and Kristin were far from objective. "Mommy!" Kristin wailed. "Do something!"

Yes, certainly. Do something.

The thought flitted through my brain, "Why don't you pray?"

I immediately rejected it, reasoning, "This kitten is obviously going to die, which really isn't uncommon for a first litter. Besides, if I pray for healing and then the cat dies, what will my kids think of God? What would it do to their faith?"

Just as quickly, the Spirit of God spoke to my spirit: "Nancy, I have not placed my reputation in your hands. I'll take care of your kids' faith. You just obey me. Pray for the kitten."

The kids readily agreed, and we laid fingers on the small corpse-like body. David, not encumbered with my adult common sense and doubts, prayed briefly and simply, asking God to heal the kitty. And that was that.

As the afternoon wore on, the kitten grew weaker. I moved it close to the mother, hoping instinct would prod Balofur to care for it. But she was still too bewildered by all the events of the day to be of much help. In spite of the lack of encouraging signs, I felt good. God's words had touched a deep place in me, and I was free to leave the whole situation in God's hands. How silly to think I was the guardian of the Almighty's reputation—that so much depended on me.

That night we put the four cats in a basket and went to bed.

The next morning all three kittens were squealing, sucking, sleeping—doing all the things normal, healthy kittens are supposed to do. Balofur seemed resigned to her new responsibilities and was mothering like an old pro. David named kitten number two "Miracle."

In the succeeding weeks Miracle's vivacity and active mischief reminded me that God's reputation was not my worry.

Of course it wouldn't be completely honest to leave this story as it is. Our family has had its share of sad pet stories, times when we prayed and, well....

Mokey came to us some years after Miracle's birth. This lively little terrier was one of the most intelligent dogs I have known. We all loved her, but she was Kristin's special pet. And her demise still tugs at our hearts. In order to keep the ants out of the food, Hal had sprayed the legs of the old kitchen cabinet with an insecticide that probably would have been illegal in the United States. Bolivian standards were more lenient, and the powerful spray did indeed take care of the ants. Unfortunately, it also took care of Mokey. We figured she had licked some of it (she was not a picky eater), because she quickly became violently ill. In spite of our fervent prayers, natural consequences played out and Mokey died.

And I think of Pancake, the funny hamster Uncle Clyde gave to David. We called him Pancake because when we petted him, he spread out all four legs and flattened down in bliss. He almost seemed to purr. But David was still learning about responsibility and had not yet made a strong connection between regular meals and his pet's well-being. Again, no amount of praying would revive Pancake, and knowing that starvation was the cause of death didn't help matters.

Although I prefer lessons learned through miraculous answers to prayer, we grew stronger as a family as we talked about the deaths of our pets, worked through the emotions, and decided to keep on talking to God.

In spite of the risks, we made the decision to involve our kids in praying for more than the healing of pets. We prayed for the healing of people, relationships, even countries. We prayed for peace in violent places. Sometimes we saw the answers and documented them in a prayer notebook. Often we observed no visible short-term results.

And sometimes the results surprised us. One Sunday morning, before Hal left on a trip to visit a church, we were praying together. Kristin, probably eight years old at the time, was feeling rebellious, not wanting to pray out loud. Hal encouraged her, and she finally just blurted out, "Help Daddy not to get killed in a car wreck today! Amen!" David laughed and Kristin burst into tears. On that note Hal drove off.

Later that night when Hal returned, he told us of nearly being run off the road by an oncoming truck. The driver had momentarily gone to sleep. It was a winding mountain road, and the mere presence of a flat place on the side to veer onto was evidence of God's care. We remembered Kristin's funny prayer, but this time without laughter. God had heard her and had honored her growing faith.

God's reputation was not ruined; our kids still trust their Savior, and they're passing it on to their children—at times praying for risky, scary stuff. I'm still learning to take my prayer clues from God. Knowing how to pray, especially with kids, can be puzzling. I'm grateful for the occasional small miracle. I love it when Christ whispers, "Pray for the cat."

The Quiet Awakening

Judith L. Butler

Judith L. Butler has published a book of poems called *Nevada Belle &*
The Forgotten Women of the West and is working on a second volume,
a memoir about travels with her father, a pastor.

Judith feels blessed to have lived in San Francisco, the Napa Valley,
and now seasonally in Palm Springs. She has one nephew, two nieces,
and four pooches: Ellie, Roxy, Toby, and Coco. Her husband, who
"really wants to be a cowboy," shoots independent films.

I GREW UP beneath the majestic eastern Sierra Nevada
mountains of California—a shy girl full of big dreams and a
very active imagination. Most could not see past the timid child
I was, but inside something was brewing. My mother sensed
that there was more to me than just a quiet, sweet girl—
perhaps because she had been shy as well as a little girl and
later as a grown woman. Mom struggled to express herself in
social situations as I did, and preferred to remain in the shadows. Our pale confidence and quiet demeanor was a fine
thread connecting us to each other.

We lived in a wonderful two-story Victorian house in the
middle of our town's Indian reservation, though we were not
of Native American descent. The Paiute tribal land ran through
the middle of the little Sierra town near the well-travelled
Highway 395. A few private homes like ours sat in between
the tribal wood and brick houses. I liked being a part of the

reservation. We loved the open fields and grassy lands around our property. My sisters and I had run of the place—a few dogs, our own little creek, and a handful of fruit trees. What more could a kid want? We built forts in the summer and put on dramatic productions for our parents in the backyard. We also played serious baseball with the two brothers across the street.

One summer day my mother softly announced that the little girl next door would be coming to visit me. I was taken aback. The dark-skinned little girl seemed rather mysterious and strange. I'd mostly seen her from a distance through the fence and the bushes between our houses, playing by herself in her yard. Her family kept to themselves. The girl was withdrawn and uncommunicative. In my young eyes she was very different from my familiar circle of friends, safe and known. She was given that frightening label of "epilepsy" in a time when little was known about the illness. Though I'm sure my mother knew more about the disease than we did as children, what we didn't fully understand terrified us. The doctors had done all they could for the young child, but in those days the medications were not as sophisticated as they are today, so the little girl continued to suffer symptoms that, to my young mind, made her even more frightening, even more unknown.

I had to wonder what my mother was thinking, inviting this strange girl to our house. But being an obedient, compliant daughter, I kept my fears silent. My mother had spoken, and I honored her wishes: The spooky girl next door would be coming over, would be touching my toys, would be breathing in my space.

I dreaded the coming afternoon playdate. How would we fill our time, me and this stranger? What if the girl had a "spell" right there on our porch? I knew my mother would be just beyond the front door, to help if necessary, but still the idea scared me. What would I do if she fell on the porch or began to bleed? What if she started to shake and didn't stop? What if I was responsible for making her seizures stop? Would I know what to do? Not rational fears, but real to me nonetheless. The most persistent fear: What if we had nothing to say to each other?

When she arrived, I noticed she wore a pretty but plain dress. Her eyes were downcast. Our time together started quietly. I was truly fearful of this great unknown. My palms sweated, and my voice felt all squeaky and high pitched. After a few minutes we began to play some games—rather awkwardly—and I grew less afraid of the girl suddenly collapsing. I relaxed some. She also seemed to develop a small bit of trust for me, her neighbor stranger. I was just as frightening to her as she was to me.

For a time on that open porch we forgot the shadows that lay between us, as children do naturally, left on their own. We were two young girls finding our way, building a bridge over unchartered waters. No one passing by our gate on that country lane could see the deep significance of the two figures, laughing and talking with each other. But even at that young age, I knew the significance was there.

Still, it seemed an ordinary day: the grasshoppers jumping high amongst the tiger lilies in the side yard, our sheep noisily calling for their supper in the back forty, and the sun shining brightly over the tall peaks of Mt. Tom.

Before we knew it the play time was over. Her father walked in stoic silence as he came to the front gate to take his daughter home. I had such a rush of mixed-up feelings stirring inside of me, as though a new cloud has passed over and all things I knew had somehow changed.

I could not seem to hold onto the old fears. The one-on-one experience had shattered my paranoia. She was a shy little girl like me; a part of me felt as though I no longer had to fear the unknown as I had before.

My mother didn't say much about that afternoon. By not making a big deal out of my playdate with a stranger, I think she allowed me even more of an epiphany. My mother acted in a gesture of peace—an offering of an outstretched hand across unknown borders.

My new muscles of compassion expanded and grew over the years. Clearly my mother sowed the first seeds of true empathy in me that afternoon, though I would not see the outcome of that initial planting for many years. It was a most simple act: a mother seeing an isolated neighbor girl and thinking her quiet middle daughter would be kind and welcoming.

Sadly, I never saw the young girl face-to-face again. Only from a distance, through the old fence that separated our two yards, did we catch glimpses of each other after that day.

My mother began to work longer hours at the little country store and my sisters and I seemed busy with various school activities. Some years later when I had gone off to college, my mother told me, in a very soft voice, that the young girl had died. My first instinct was to cry, thinking had our lives been less complicated, we might have gotten to know each other better. That our mutual fears and imagined differences did not stand in the way of our becoming friends for a day, and—had circumstances been different—might not have prevented us from being companions for a lifetime, however long (or short) that life may have been.

To Tell the Truth

Paula J. Hampton

Paula Hampton's Quaker roots sprawl deep, and stretch back to colonial days. But she sometimes wonders if recessive Mennonite genes lurk somewhere in her past, for baking and quilting are two of her main hobbies. She also enjoys reading, finding personal narratives and memoir particularly fascinating; sometimes she even writes her own.

In addition to parenting three young-adult children, Paula works part time as an editor for Barclay Press. She and her husband, Larry, live on the outskirts of Newberg, Oregon.

JOSEPH PLOPS down in the chair across the room from where I sit opening the mail. We'd walked in the door just a few minutes earlier; I can hear Joseph's older sisters search for an after-school snack in the kitchen.

"So, how was your first week as a first grader?" I ask, tearing open an envelope. I try to keep my voice casual. Last year, during kindergarten, Joseph struggled to be away from home even half a day. Now, with his first week of all-day school attendance under his belt, I wonder if he feels more confident, less anxious.

Joseph draws his knees up to his chest, wraps his arms around his shins, and drops his head. "I don't want to tell you," he mumbles.

My normally chatty boy does not want to talk. He's always been tenderhearted, and is usually very open with me. What happened at school to make him shut down like this? I give him my full attention: "Did something happen today?" I ask. "Tell me," I demand, in my now-we're-all-business mom voice.

Joseph raises his head slightly; looks at me. "I said we went to Alaska," he confesses.

"What?" I try to make sense of his admission.

"We had to say what we did this summer, and I said we went to Alaska," he explains, hiding his face in his arms again.

"Joseph! We did not go to Alaska; you know that! You told your teacher a lie?"

Joseph looks up at me, pain on his face, tears in his eyes. I'm not sure what to do. Larry and I have always tried to model straightforward, honest words and deeds. We value our Quaker heritage of integrity and "plain speech." When a cashier fails to ring up the laundry detergent or dog food on the bottom rack of the grocery cart, I haul the kids back into the store with me to pay for it. When we find a twenty-dollar bill in the school parking lot, we turn it in to the office. "It's not ours, and someone may come looking for it," I tell the kids. "It might be someone's lunch money." When I misspeak or misrepresent facts, or come on too strongly in conversations or in meetings, I swallow my pride and apologize, seeking reconciliation and understanding. The kids—on several occasions—have heard me repeat a line my parents spoke during my own childhood: "Tell us the truth about what happened. You're going to be in more trouble if you don't." I wonder what could have prompted my sensitive, conscientious young son to tell an outright lie.

I look at the clock. Not quite 3:30. "Get your shoes on," I instruct. "We're going back to school and you're going to tell Mrs. Grant the truth. I'm not going to let a child of mine get away with not telling the truth!"

"No, mom! Please..." Joseph protests, whimpering a little. But he obeys anyway, and after a brief explanation to the girls ("What? Joseph, you lied?"), we drive the three miles back to school.

We find Mrs. Grant in the first-grade classroom, stapling student artwork to the bulletin board. Each piece of construction paper is shaped like a large hot air balloon, with a student drawing and a few sentences typed out: "What I did this summer."

Mrs. Grant looks surprised to see us. "What can I do for you?" she asks.

"Well, Joseph has something he needs to tell you," I prompt, standing behind my son, my hands firmly on his shoulders.

"Go on," I say to Joseph. "Tell her...."

Joseph looks up at me, then over to his teacher. "We didn't go to Alaska," he ventures quietly.

"He didn't tell you the truth about his summer," I explain.

Mrs. Grant stifles a chuckle, I can tell. She begins to laugh it off. But I don't want this teachable moment to become just another cute and funny classroom story the teachers share in the staff room. I want Joseph to learn a lesson. Here. Now.

From where I stand behind Joseph's back, I send Mrs. Grant a nonverbal message: *Come down hard on him, please*, I mouth. *Make him do the assignment over again.* She seems to catch on.

"Well, Joseph. Let's find your hot air balloon," she says, searching the wall until she finds a drawing of a fishing boat out on the water, with Joseph's dictated words underneath.

We went to Alaska.
My dad and I went fishing.
We slept on a boat.
We caught lots of fish.
It was fun!

Mrs. Grant pulls out the staples and hands Joseph his project. She walks to her desk, finds a blank hot air balloon paper and hands it to him. He sits down at a table and goes to work.

This time he draws a picture of himself swimming. "We went to the Carlton pool to go swimming," he dictates. Mrs. Grant staples his new paper into the empty spot on the bulletin board.

"Thanks for coming back and telling me the truth," she says. "It's important to always tell the truth."

Joseph nods. "Can we go now, Mom?" he asks. "I'm hungry."

"Yep. We'll see you Monday, Mrs. Grant!" *And thanks so much,* I mouth. Mrs. Grant's eyes twinkle in response.

"Good-bye, Joseph," she says as we walk out the door.

On the way home I ask Joseph why he felt he needed to make something up about his summer.

"All we did was stay home and go swimming," he replies. "That just didn't sound very cool. Going to Alaska sounded cool."

A few weeks later I share Joseph's story with the women at my Bible study meeting. They laugh. A few feel sorry for Joseph. "You made him go back, Paula?" they chide. So I tell them that I want to communicate to Joseph just how highly I value truth-telling.

Still, I wonder if I've come down on Joseph too hard. Did I humiliate him, scar him for life? Or did he learn an important lesson with the stakes still low? Honesty and integrity run deep in our family and I expect Joseph to carry on that heritage. Does my pride drive that desire? Or does a deeply imbedded truth trait move me?

All this gets me thinking. I begin to wonder if there might be an "honesty gene" in the family lineage. I ask around. My brother tells me how Grandpa, when faced with losing his farm during the Great Depression, refused to bad-mouth the men from the bank who came to repossess his horses — even when they took the colts too. Grandpa knew they were within their rights, and he was careful to protect their reputations even though financial strain could have made him bitter. His restraint made an impression on his young sons. Uncle Harold tells me how Grandpa's sister, a woman known for strong language at times, once accused her brother of being "too damn honest." That got his boys' attention!

Uncle Morris, who sold farm machinery, became known for dealing forthrightly with customers. At his memorial service, men from the community — many the family didn't know — spoke of Morris's integrity and compassion, and confirmed a legacy of truthfulness and honesty.

My own father was known for his plain speech. Perhaps it was due in part to his journalism training — "just the facts" — but Dad held to his word. He worked hard to keep confidential information confidential. In discussions he often spoke out on behalf of the "other side" of an argument, helping a board or committee to stay on task, refusing to engage in political tactics that might undermine an organization's integrity.

I discuss my heritage of integrity with a few close friends. Exactly what is it about our family that perpetuates such honesty? "There's no pretense," one says. "What you see is what you get."

"It's 'plain speech,'" says another. "You have opinions and share them straightforwardly." There's no guessing. No wondering. No swaying back and forth depending on whether one speaks privately or publicly.

I think about that as I look at my son. He's sixteen now, and we can laugh about his imaginary trip to Alaska. Making things right with his teacher may have seemed harsh at the time, but the experience served Joseph well. That lesson about honesty—along with our modeling, stories he heard growing up, and maybe even that "honesty gene"—are like rods of rebar laid in concrete. They provide the strong foundation that's helped Joseph grow into a young man of integrity. He's surrounded by family members who speak honestly; he follows a long line of "plain speakers." And even if he doesn't always get it right, Joseph knows we trust him to speak the truth and to deal truthfully with others—just as his forbears did.

Blessed are the Peacemakers

"Do not be overcome by evil,
but overcome evil with good."

Romans 12:21 ESV

Dixie Chicks Gospel: Taking the Long Way

Lisa Weaver

Lisa Weaver is the author of *Praying with Our Feet* (Herald Press, 2005), a picture book that explores the way in which a young child and her church community can witness to peace.

Lisa is a third-grade teacher in a public school, and an active member of her Mennonite church. Happily married for nearly two decades, Lisa and her husband are the proud parents of two teenage boys.

I DROPPED OFF my two boys in their respective schools — first grade for my older son, preschool for my littlest fellow. I was planning to spend a quiet morning at home, sipping my favorite tea and studying for the music-theory class I was taking at a local college. As I began the short drive back to my house, I absent-mindedly flipped on the car radio. Only much later would I realize how what I heard in the next few minutes would impact my thoughts and influence conversations with my boys over the next several years. It was March 20, 2003, and I listened in disbelief to the announcement that the United States had just invaded Iraq.

My country has started a war? I thought in horror. Coldness settled over my body. My heart felt like a heavy stone.

Perhaps I should have expected this turn of events, but I had instead been harboring hope that the war could be avoided. Temperate voices from across the nation had been calling for caution and seemingly daily reports of vibrant protests had filled the news. There had been demonstrations in my own city, in the nation's capital, and in many locations across the country. I had been encouraged by editorials saying there had never been such a widespread "conventional" peace movement, filled with minivan-driving, stroller-pushing parents. The protestors were not just a handful of whackos on the leftist fringe. "Has no one been listening?" I asked my steering wheel.

As I neared my driveway I thought briefly about the half notes and key signatures in my current course assignment. But my mind was preoccupied with the other side of the world where bombs were dropping—bombs that carried the insignia of my country—and the idea of studying turned my stomach.

Responding to a vague but pressing need to "do something," I did not turn into my driveway but rather drove on. My thoughts floated to a three-woman, country-pop-rock band from Texas called the Dixie Chicks. My awareness of the Dixie Chicks was only a few days old—from a story my husband had told me about their lead singer, Natalie Maines. Maines and her group had been thrust into the political spotlight because of an offhand comment Maines made about the president. Just ten days earlier, during a March 10 concert in London, Maines had said from stage that the Dixie Chicks did not want the war or the violence and that they were "ashamed the president of the United States is from Texas." The media picked up this remark, and harsh condemnation quickly followed. The women in the group, Natalie Maines and sisters Emily Robison and Marty Maguire, were branded as "unpatriotic" and a disgrace to their nation.

Though most certainly my action would not register on anyone's list of the most profound war protests of this century, I decided I would buy a Dixie Chicks CD as my personal protest against the invasion that had just begun.

I pulled into the parking lot of a bookstore near my home, thinking of a song by Patty Shelley that we had sung in church a couple weeks earlier. One line kept repeating itself for me: "Strengthen the hands of those who work for peace." Quite frankly, my only knowledge of the Dixie Chicks was one media-generated story, and I didn't know if what the Dixie Chicks did could be called "working for peace." I had a perception, however, that they spoke against warring actions, and on this morning, at this moment, that was good enough. I wondered if their marketing department would notice my purchase on this day and correctly register it as a war protest.

I walked through the front door of the bookstore, and "God Bless America" in full orchestral splendor assaulted my ears. Neurons fired alarmingly in my brain. My skin sizzled. The coldness and heaviness I had experienced in the car were instantaneously replaced by white-hot anger. I strode to the customer service counter directly in front of me, eyes blazing. "Who put on this music?" I demanded loudly, hands raised in disbelief, restraining the impulse to sweep all the books off the counter in a dramatic gesture. "We are killing people, and we're playing 'God Bless America'?"

The clerk behind the service desk stepped back. "I think they control that upstairs," he said.

I bounded up the stairs and approached a second service desk. "Who is in charge here?" I asked again, once more noting aloud the vulgarity of juxtaposing God's blessing and this war.

The attendant's eyes quickly darted side to side before she leaned in close and whispered, "I don't like it either."

Perhaps she had studied conflict de-escalation techniques at some point in her life because her empathetic acknowledgment of my words had an immediately calming effect on me. I was now able to ignore the music and state more quietly, "I am here to buy a Dixie Chicks CD."

I was soon on my way out of the store, newly purchased CD in hand. I paused at the front door, suddenly aware that the airwaves were silent. No music played in the store at all. When did that happen? The thought occurred to me that perhaps it was only the gap between soundtracks, but I didn't wait to find out.

And so the Dixie Chicks women entered my house via their *Home* album. I listened to them as my boys jumped and bopped around my feet in the kitchen. I heard the lyrical words express anger and resolve. I grew to love their gutsy harmonies, lively banjo picking, beautiful fiddle lines, and strong guitar. I marveled at Natalie Maines's ability to pass between her strident lower register and her perfectly pitched, high gentle twang. The energy in the songs increased my blood flow. I recalled my father's words when, as a young teenager I had asked him if he thought it was ethical for a musician to devote his or her life to music when there was so much trouble in the world to address. I sensed now why he answered "yes."

Perhaps because the Dixie Chicks had joined the ranks (albeit somewhat by accident) of those who challenged authority, listening to their music made me think of my favorite New Testament stories: when Jesus dared to walk through instead of around the despised land of Samaria, even stopping to share words and water with a woman at a well; when Jesus broke a law by healing a man's withered hand on the Sabbath instead of waiting until the next day; when Jesus threw the money-changers out of the temple to protest the corruption of temple practices. Though I was not so simplistic as to think that the lives of the Dixie Chicks were the model after which I would like to tailor all my actions, I distinctly preferred to line myself up with them rather than to stand beside the military machine churning out systematic death and destruction in a distant country.

My husband and I struggled with how to explain war—the war in Iraq, any war—to our sons. Whenever we talked about the fact of war, we tried to accompany our description with stories of people who were working to end the war, or who were working to help those caught within the conflict. I told the boys that one of the reasons I liked the Dixie Chicks was that they spoke out against the war. The boys' loving little hearts agreed with me that war was a bad idea.

For two years I drove to work, hearing frequent radio reports about two, twelve, twenty-five or more Iraqi people killed, as well as smaller numbers of U.S. soldiers. It made me sad to think that for me they were just numbers tumbling out of the radio, but to the families of those killed it was gut-wrenching news that could not be cast aside or turned off. I was dumbfounded to see deep cuts in funding and programming in our local school district, while simultaneously hearing that Congress was approving the spending of *billions* more on military actions in Iraq and Afghanistan.

I watched news reports that showed former fans of the Dixie Chicks piling up their CDs and driving tractors over them. Many country music radio stations blackballed their music. Some DJs who played it anyway were suspended. The state legislature of South Carolina voted a resolution of censure and asked the Chicks to apologize. The Dixie Chicks received serious death threats.

"Are you sorry you said it?" asked Steve Kroft in his *60 Minutes* interview with the Chicks.

"Sorry for what?" shot back Natalie Maines. She shook her head and fixed him with a deliberately perplexed and sharply disbelieving stare. "Sorry that I didn't want people to die? Sorry that I didn't want my country to go to war?"

I talked with my boys about the fact that sometimes we need to take a stand for peace, even if doing so is unpopular.

We shared stories about family and community members who performed alternative service assignments rather than join the military. The boys lent their hand strength to stapling and distributing peace signs, an action organized by members of our church. We were humbled by the bravery of the Christian Peacemaker Teams members who traveled to Iraq.

One day my husband announced that the Dixie Chicks had a new album coming out soon. "Are you going to get it, Mom?" my boys wanted to know.

I assured them I would. A few days later, when I saw a man in front of me at a checkout counter holding a copy of their new CD, I ducked out of line to go back and find my own to purchase. I quickly located *Taking the Long Way*, but did not stop to examine the cover of the album until I reached my car in the parking lot. Once there, I was pleased to see that the Chicks continued to wear high heels and ample eye makeup. They still looked like the women on the cover of my *Home* album, and I applauded their sense of identity. I took off the shrink wrap and popped the disc into the car stereo so I could listen to it on my way home.

Shortly thereafter I was forced to ask myself whether or not it was safe to drive with tears streaming down my face. I did at least have to admit that trying to read the eight-point font to examine the lyrics while on a busy street would not be a good idea. I mentally distanced myself from the music. "*Six strong hands on the steering wheel,*" Natalie had sung on track one, and I took this as not only a statement of agency by the Chicks, but as a personal admonition to myself to pay attention to my driving.

I had not been prepared for the power of the songs. Written by the Chicks themselves, the lyrics revealed the depths to which they were originally shaken by the harsh public outcry against them, and the strength and understanding which eventually grew instead of faltered. I needed time and a place where I could close my eyes and let tears fall. My husband and boys became accustomed to the fact that I needed a Kleenex when I listened to my new CD.

We checked the official Web site of the Dixie Chicks, hoping to find a nearby concert in the *Taking the Long Way* tour. Unfortunately, the venue closest to us was in a neighboring state and going would be more of an undertaking than we felt prepared for. We waffled back and forth, trying to weigh costs of time and money against deep feelings. We avoided actually purchasing tickets, though I kept the date of this nearest concert in my head. And, when on that date I called my husband at 10:00 a.m., I did not have to explain what I meant when I said, "I think I need to go."

"I'll be home in an hour," he replied, and I knew this was one reason I loved him.

I rallied the boys, who thought a last-minute trip was a great lark. They ran through the house with me, choosing toys for the car and helping me gather snacks and water bottles. I tossed clothes for all of us in a bag, and by the time my husband arrived, we were nearly ready to go. When we were actually on the road, we had seven hours to drive five. I felt the past weeks of indecision melting away, as I was now on my way to "meet" the three women I had come to know through words and music.

I thought of my boys in the car beside me, chattering happily, pointing out cows and horses in fields. What would they remember of the war? Of this trip? Of the music Mom played in the kitchen?

I recalled I had recently heard someone important say that the United States would never leave Iraq—that we're building bases, and that we plan to stay. And "Stay the course," the president appeared fond of saying. But my antidote for this creeping resignation was to remember the flashing eyes and sharpened voice of my dear Mennonite mother-in-law. In nearly two decades of knowing her, I had never heard her raise her voice, until I had lamented one day that the war was happening in our name. "Not in *my* name," she'd said, with a defiant lift of the chin.

And that is why, when my boys looked around at the concert and one of them leaned over to me and whispered, "There aren't many boys here, Mom. Is it okay for *us* to be here?" I said, "Absolutely," and took their hands.

As the music filled the arena, I looked at my boys who were quietly drinking in the experience. I cannot control their future thoughts and decisions, but I hope that they will remember — or at least sometime figure out — that our lives are expressions of our convictions. I hope my boys will remember — and reflect upon — the fact that their parents were not in support of the war. I hope that they will remember — and understand why — it was important for their mom to be a part of a voice bigger than her own. And I hope one day they will each sing the songs in their hearts. I look forward to hearing what that will be. I hope, with the Dixie Chicks, for "more love, more joy and laughter…I hope we can all live more fearlessly."

The Quagmire in My Son's Backpack

Lora Jost

Lora Jost is the mother of an eight-year-old boy. She is a freelance artist whose work draws attention to mundane, whimsical, and urgent life experiences. She is also an illustrator and community arts educator, currently teaching at the Lawrence (Kansas) Arts Center.

She coauthored *Kansas Murals: A Traveler's Guide* (University Press of Kansas, 2006), which received a Kansas Notable Book Award, and has an essay, "Kindergarten Boogy-Bunny," on Mamazine.com.

MY SON'S first day of school was over. Like most parents, I looked through his backpack at day's end, and what I found caused within me an intense period of reflection. His teacher had sent home a folder with a form to sign for completed homework, and a photocopied *First Grade Handbook* that explained classroom procedures and a behavior plan involving a big construction paper stoplight. Mrs. Berry explained in the handbook that her husband was in the National Guard deployed in Kosovo, and that this year the first-grade class would be writing letters to American soldiers there.

My heart sank. I was not expecting this. I had hoped Mrs. Berry would be a good fit for Cole. She always appeared gentle and relaxed, less "by the book" than the other two teachers, but letters to soldiers? Not a good fit—not for me.

I called my husband, Alex, and read to him from the handbook, visualizing Mrs. Berry wrapped in a flag talking to the first graders about soldiers serving our country. I imagined Mrs. Berry holding a torch, telling our young sons and daughters about the American soldiers fighting in Iraq for our freedom. I didn't want my son exposed to this. I didn't want him to think that being a soldier was cool.

Alex wasn't pleased either, but was more confident than I that we could work something out with Mrs. Berry. If the kids must write letters to soldiers, he reasoned, then to be fair the class must also write letters to conscientious objectors and to victims of war. We could help her with that. Alex would send an e-mail immediately.

But then I said, "Let's wait." We both decided to sit on our concern for a while.

Our dilemma arose from our upbringing. "Love your enemy," "Pray for those who persecute you," and "Turn the other cheek" were teachings that ran deep in our childhood communities. We were both raised in the Mennonite pacifist tradition. For five hundred years our ancestors did everything they could to keep from being conscripted into the military, including emigrating from country to country, eventually to North America. Pacifism runs deep in our soul.

Mennonites are Anabaptists, called this because they baptize adult believers instead of infants. They believe that no one should be forced to embrace the Christian faith or to kill others for their country's sake. Many early sixteenth-century Anabaptists were persecuted, tortured, and martyred for these beliefs. Because of this, Mennonites learned to keep their heads down and became known as "the quiet in the land."

As Alex and I sought education and jobs, we moved away from Mennonite country. We also moved away from the church, yet our Mennonite backgrounds that emphasized pacifism, service, cultural heritage, and community remained core parts of our identity.

They were not core for Cole, however, and maybe never would be in the same way they were for us. Cole was growing up in Lawrence, Kansas, a liberal university town, and he wasn't steeped in everyday connections to "our people." The families we had become close to through Cole's community nursery school and elementary school were diverse yet close-knit and open-minded. These were people and values we cherished. Even so, it would take time with them to build the trust we needed to feel comfortable sharing candidly about our backgrounds. The father of one of Cole's friends, for example, was a career military officer. It was one thing to be politically liberal (and this officer was), and quite another to hold the anti-war views of my earlier home community. Sometimes this kind of difference left us feeling lonely, like this circle of friends didn't really know us.

Cole hit first grade and the soldier pen-pal project in August of 2008, when the United States was engaged in two Middle Eastern wars. Alex and I didn't talk much with Cole about the wars, but neither did we fully shield him from our conversations about them. We told him as a matter of fact that the United States was at war and that war was wrong. We did our best to demonstrate our views in the community.

During the buildup to the Iraq war, Alex and I had participated in weekly anti-war vigils for a year, sponsored by the Lawrence Coalition for Peace and Justice. We took family snapshots at various peace events with our little son in tow. Though we did not protest with this in mind, maybe documenting our family's long-standing opposition to war would someday help Cole if he ever needed to claim conscientious-objector status in front of a draft board.

When the Iraq War started, I participated in a quiet protest called a "die-in," and Alex and Cole came along. I felt self-conscious lying on the cold sidewalk with a group of twenty or so others, pretending to be dead. But we wanted to dramatize the fact that war kills people. We wanted to speak the unspeakable. During the die-in, Alex held Cole in a baby sling and kept him from seeing the action, yet Cole was close enough to hear the wails of the actors. Cole imitated these sounds, and his high-pitched mewls brought home the war in a deeply personal way. In that moment my child was every child vulnerable to the ravages of war. And in that moment I was dead, unable to answer his cries.

When I was writing letters of concern about the war to legislators, Cole was four. He wrote a letter too, to President Bush, saying, "If war can stop it would be happy for us." He got a letter back from the White House that said, "Your generation is growing up in a historic time when freedom is on the march, and America is proud to lead the armies of liberation." Cole also got an eight-by-eleven-inch glossy photo of the president.

At age five, Cole wrote another letter to the Oval Office that simply said, "War is not okay." Somehow, the idea that war was not okay had taken hold.

Now at age six, he would be writing letters to soldiers. Alex and I knew we needed to say something to Mrs. Berry, but explaining our concerns would mean admitting, as politely as we could, that we have a problem with soldiers because the job of soldiers in times of war is to kill people, and we believe that killing is wrong. Could we be this honest with Cole's teacher? That was our real dilemma.

By now we were backing off the idea of placing additional demands on Mrs. Berry's assignment. Maybe we could simply ask her some questions. What if, for example, Cole blurted out "War is wrong." Would she say that he was wrong? What if Cole asked "Don't soldiers kill people?" Would she say no? Would she say they only kill bad people?

We had no idea if Cole would ask any questions like these. We had talked with him enough about war being wrong, and we were certain that the soldier pen-pal assignment could be thoroughly confusing. We wanted Mrs. Berry to respect his difference, but we didn't want her to treat him differently, and given that, we began to wonder if we should say anything at all.

Alex and I knew that being different could feel uncomfortable. While the insular Mennonite communities we grew up in made Mennonite difference feel normal, we were also keenly aware that Mennonites were sometimes viewed as weird by the mainstream. When one young Mennonite from my home church was drafted, he went to jail instead of Vietnam. His choice was revered in our little town of North Newton, made up mostly of Mennonites linked with the college located there. The larger town of Newton was just across the tracks, where young men were drafted and went to war. Because Mennonite college students protested the war, antagonism toward Mennonites ran deep. One conservative pastor from Newton even outfitted his old white station wagon with loudspeakers and drove around North Newton blaring insults at our kind.

This was in my mind when I wondered if our talking with Mrs. Berry would help or hurt. Cole was still so tender and impressionable. Would talking with her avert a difficult situation, or create a new one?

I asked some friends what they thought. One, who grew up with hippie parents and was homeschooling her boy, said "Welcome to the public schools!" A Quaker friend was appalled by the soldier project and said at the very least the kids should also write letters to people who have served their country in other ways. Another friend, an ex-Catholic whose daughter was in Cole's class, also had some concerns about the project. She asked, "Who are these presumably young men who will be writing letters to our children, and what if they say something inappropriate?" Despite her concerns, my friend thought she could process any fallout more easily with her six-year-old than she could with Mrs. Berry.

She did caution me against using the words *conscientious objector*. *Pacifist* was less political, she said, more spiritual. And *pacifist* is what her Vietnam War veteran father called himself. She suggested that the religious component of my pacifism might come in handy if we decided to talk with Mrs. Berry, who we both perceived as a conservative Christian, based on the name of the college she'd attended. But I told her, "I can't speak that language any more with any kind of integrity."

In many ways this was the heart of the problem. How could we explain ourselves? Our core pacifist beliefs were based on the shared practice of a religious community that in many ways we were no longer a part of. We were taking a different path. Some would say we were assimilating. But on this question we definitely were not. We wanted to raise our son as a fervent pacifist, but without that community support, we were floundering.

As we struggled, we settled into a comfortable sort of inaction. But our feelings about the pen-pal project also came and went in visceral waves. It didn't take much to figure out why: In 1980, Alex was among a small group of eighteen-year-old Mennonite pacifists in the Newton area who struggled with President Carter's reinstatement of draft registration. A military threat to the Soviet Union for invading Afghanistan could have led to forced conscription down the line. Alex chose to oppose draft registration by not registering. A felony. He was prosecuted for it.

It was clear that the government was going to prosecute only a few vocal protestors, and Alex's case finally came to trial. By then he and I were in love. It was summertime, a year after we had met in college when I was just a freshman. Alex was a senior. It was a stressful time—not knowing what would happen to him. Even so, we tried to plan our futures together. What a relief it was when his case was thrown out in a compromise and the whole ordeal was over.

This story was our secret. People "circle the wagons" around their scary times, and we had been closeting this for years.

It is tough in any case to be "out of the closet" as a pacifist, and it is difficult for me to write about my problem with soldiers. Some people will find that raising moral questions about the work of soldiers is un-patriotic. Some will think I believe soldiers are bad people. Some will decry pacifists as naïve, unrealistic, and unappreciative. But we aren't.

Maybe it would have been easier to talk with Mrs. Berry about our problem with soldiers if she were an impersonal authority like the president, the pope, or the police. But she wasn't that kind of authority. She was a young teacher who was pregnant, and her husband was overseas with the military. As one friend noted, "She's gotta be scared." Alex and I didn't want Mrs. Berry to feel as if we didn't understand her family's sacrifice, and we didn't want to add any more stress to her life than she was already feeling.

By November we had said nothing to Mrs. Berry about the soldier pen-pal project. Was it still happening? It was totally off our radar.

Then one day Cole brought home a worksheet called "Keeping Our Country Free." It included a drawing he had made of a soldier. The directions read, "Draw someone from the military in that person's uniform. It could be a friend, family member, or someone you studied. Write why you are thankful for that person." That day Cole also brought home a copy of the letter that a soldier, based in Kosovo, had written to his class. The letter included short answers to questions from specific kids, though no answers were for Cole.

I pulled the materials from Cole's backpack and started reading them out loud to Alex. Cole was nearby and speedily blurted out, "Soldiers help people! They only kill people when they absolutely have to."

I was stunned. "Who told you that?" Alex and I asked simultaneously.

Then Alex said to Cole, "Soldiers fight and use weapons and kill people, and that's not good."

Now Cole was stunned. "We have to do it, everybody has to do it," Cole said. He was emotional and defensive. Alex told Cole he understood that Cole had to do the assignment, but what soldiers do isn't good.

"We have a difference of opinion with your teacher," I added. But Cole was agitated, enough so that we both backed off. Way off. We were handling this badly. Alex and I looked at each other.

"We're gonna need to work on this," Alex said.

The soldier pen-pal project had come to roost. Cole wanted to believe his teacher. He wanted to believe that what soldiers do is good. The soldier Cole drew was his friend's father, the military officer, a good man who was our friend too. The whole thing was wildly confusing.

Our conversation continued, and Cole told us excitedly that soldiers play a lot of professional sports. No doubt we looked intrigued. What the soldier actually said in his letter was that to pass the time they play sports, including basketball, volleyball, and softball. The soldier also said—in language intended for a six-year-old—that the U.S. military was in Kosovo because Kosovo was trying to gain independence. The military was there to help Kosovo and to make sure "the peace is kept." Most of the questions he answered were about his daily life and the military base where he lived. He also said that there were good things and bad things about the army. On the good side, "We get to shoot off different types of guns and people have a lot of respect for the military." On the bad side, the service included much waiting around and doing *useless things.*

A week later my friend Pia dropped off her son, who was in Cole's class, at our house for a play date. I was making French toast and invited her in for a chat. Pia said, "By the way, did you happen to see that letter from the soldier?"

I jumped in. "The guns part?"

"Yes!" she exclaimed.

That launched a big discussion. We talked and speculated and wondered and exclaimed. She was mostly concerned that Mrs. Berry had so blithely passed on the comment about the guns to a group of six- and seven-year-olds. Pia's son had drawn a picture of Pia's grandfather in uniform. He had been drafted to fight in World War II. She admitted to knowing little about the situation in Kosovo, but felt what was happening in Iraq and Afghanistan was completely different than what her grandfather had gone through.

I shared with her my family history (sans the prosecution of my husband), and that I was proud that my ancestors had been conscientious objectors. I showed her a children's book by Alice Walker called *Why War Is Never a Good Idea.*

Pia noted that parent-teacher conferences were coming up. We were both fired up about the weapons comment and re-solved to speak about this with Mrs. Berry at our conferences. I later talked with Alex about our plan, and he agreed with it.

When our allotted time with the teacher arrived, Mrs. Berry greeted Alex and me warmly and spoke about Cole with affection. She shared Cole's academic progress and listened to our educational concerns. Mrs. Berry said she would give birth in December, and that she hoped her husband would be home for a couple of weeks then to be with her and their new baby.

When our time was nearly through, Alex and I looked at each other. The soldier pen-pal project had sparked some real soul searching on our part. The project had renewed our pacifist commitment and provided the occasion for our first serious conversations with Cole and our friends about these principles. But face-to-face with Mrs. Berry, we could see her as a human being, and instead of confronting her we kept our heads down and thanked her for her teaching.

We said good-bye and left. Teaching Cole about pacifism in the context of our lives and community will take constant attention and intention. There are no static rules for this practice. Sometimes it makes sense to write a letter to the president, participate in a die-in, or even break the law. But sometimes confrontation is not right either. We're still not sure we did the right thing. There is no easy answer. Staying true to our pacifist heritage will always be a struggle. And maybe that struggle, rather than a simple answer, is what we can hope to pass on to our son.

Cat on a
Hot Ride's Roof

Willi Tranmer

Because a family's battle with the stigma of diseases like mental illness and fetal alcohol syndrome are both private and never over, all names have been changed.

Willi Tranmer's essays and fiction have been published in journals such as *New Letters*, *Sundog*, *The Southeast Review*, *River Styx*, *Buffalo Carp*, *Rhubarb*, *With*, and Center for Mennonite Writing's *CMW Journal*. Willi has been a Milton Fellow in fiction (Seattle Pacific University), as well as a Starr Fellowship winner, and a Laity Lodge writer-in-residence. Willi is also a Best New Stories from the South winner (Algonquin), a winner of the Pirate's Alley William Faulkner Prize for the novel finalist, a James Jones First Novel Prize finalist, and a Bellwether Prize finalist ("Literature for Social Change," sponsored by HarperCollins and Barbara Kingsolver). She has won the Heartland Fiction Prize (New Letters) and was a finalist for Scribner's Best of the Fiction Workshops and the AWP Writers Award.

Willi's children have grown up beautifully, but Willi herself is still working on that.

"GIVE her back."

As if to emphasize his point, our new pediatrician stepped back, hands up in surrender, like he thought he was auditioning for a Scorsese film.

That was it.

That was the extent of his professional pediatric wisdom.

I had come by bus on a hot, sunny day, my two-year-old Tim sitting beside me, his hand and mine stroking six-week-old Livia's forehead. We half sung, half whispered "Puff the magic dragon lived by the sea . . . " and "The Itsy-Bitsy Spider" over and over to her, while she cried without stopping—the most plaintive little cry I'd ever heard. People on the bus were getting restless by the time we disembarked.

At six weeks old, Livia came to us, her third home in six weeks after two previous home placements, already showing severe signs of withdrawal from some unidentified substance. Livia was our first child to enter the family through a "special needs" adoption. As Tim, our first and only biological child, turned two, my husband, Michael, and I had gotten cocky. Obviously, we were very good at this parenting thing. Terrible twos? Please. We never heard from them. This Tim was pretty nice. Not yet potty trained, he was already a genuinely low-key guy. Not demanding, never petulant, virtually always cooperative, hilarious, and as a bonus, cute. Oh yeah. We were born for this.

My husband and I had both worked with people with disabilities before we were married, and both long had concerns about the many children who never get adopted, never get a family they can call their own. It felt like a no-brainer. So within two years we were a racially integrated family, and Tim had two baby sisters with genetic psychiatric and behavioral disabilities. Livia was the first to arrive.

The challenge that brought us on a two-transfer bus ride in a St. Louis heat wave was that Livia couldn't stop crying.

*   *   *

We had endured the fumes of three different buses to come to our new doctor's office so we could find out why Livia cried all the time—I mean, *all* the time. She and I slept downstairs to cozy up on the living room floor some nights. I rubbed her back and we shared earphones playing Mozart softly, in an attempt to soothe her and also to let the other two upstairs get some sleep. We understood this had been a problem with her two previous home placements. She had bonded to her crib. She was deemed "untouchable."

Some forms of drug withdrawal give babies a heightened tactile sensitivity so that touching and even affection are unpleasant; so is direct eye contact—all things that every baby also needs. So they cry when they don't get it, then cry harder when they do. They begin to associate tenderness, affection, and parental love with pain and discomfort. A cruel little catch-22. So, you know, you miss enough sleep, you hope your sharp, expensive-looking new pediatrician might have some suggestions to help her stop crying through most of each day.

His best swing at bat?

He put his hands up in the air, stepped away from the table, and said, "Give her back. There's nothing you're going to be able to do, and it's only going to get worse."

*   *   *

I left his office baffled and angry. *Give her back? Okay,* **that** *was helpful.*

Naturally, we found a new doctor. But the thing that haunted me over and over again for years is that despite my anger and disgust with this physician, both of his predictions were true for the first nineteen years: There *was* nothing we could do to help her, and it *did* only get worse. She had committed violence against others "with a deadly weapon" by the time she was ten, and by the time she was eleven she was in the judicial system and ordered into residential treatment (fortunately, she was already there by her psychiatrist's prescription, so it wasn't a sudden shock).

Livia carried mental illness on both sides of her biological family's history, and when she first came home to us, she was also demonstrating signs of being exposed to drugs in utero and signs of infant drug withdrawal.

* * *

Our second daughter, Helena, has fetal alcohol syndrome (FAS), with mild cerebral palsy and learning disabilities. Many adults and children with FAS cannot learn moral lessons and cannot retain social lessons. Instead, they often tend to make the same amoral or immoral—and sometimes criminal—choices, and can continue to behave recklessly in social situations, thriving on tension, drama, fantastic stories, and continually trusting all the wrong sorts of people, even committing crimes for them—over and over again.

Imagine the worst drunk you've ever seen. Brain temporarily impaired, that person makes mistakes he or she would never make sober, emotionally committing to really bad ideas. A baby exposed to alcohol in utero has those same brain cells destroyed before those cells develop—and so the cells simply don't develop. She's trapped in the dead-drunk world before she is even born.

* * *

Fetal alcohol, babies exposed to drugs—each case is unique, and not everyone experiences the same thing, so I can only speak to our experience. We experienced all these effects and more.

We were told we were foolish and reckless before we adopted children with these particular forms of disability.

We were told we were reckless afterward.

The most frustrating (no—enraging) critiques were those that came from individuals who assumed my daughters' "bad behaviors" were either a result of their being black, or a result of being black in a white family, cutting them absolutely no slack for being born with multiple genetic mental illnesses, plus drugs and alcohol in utero.

"Do white babies in white families always escape inheriting mental illness? Do drugs and alcohol have no effect on charming white babies?" I wanted to scream. And then, of course, there were the glares from strangers, of both races, because we were an integrated family. This, in the face of the fact that children of minority races languish in institutions or are shunted from one foster home to the next.

In retrospect, I sometimes think I should have screamed a little *more*, but instead, our saving grace—the best thing we did—was surround ourselves with supportive, positive, enthusiastic good friends. Of both races.

The most harshly voiced warnings (or accusations) we got, though, were those that said it wasn't fair to our oldest, Tim, our biological child, to have done this to him—to have given him such an unusual household. It made me wonder: Does that mean it *would* be fair if the girls were our biological issue? If we feel it's a mistake to welcome fragile children willingly, then what are we saying to those thrust on us by fate? I would think that those parents who have had no choice would object to those who told us we were not being fair to Tim.

Yet when I looked at Tim, kind and sweet as ever with these challenging little sisters, my heart ached. Maybe they were right. Maybe I should not have done this to him. But my heart broke for all three at the same time. What had I done? Who could I really help anyway, as just a plain old mom?

One complaint made me laugh.

I remember sitting on a swing in the dark, looking back at the brightly lit windows of my home. The violence associated with Livia's severe mental illness was taking over more of our family times until restraining a violent child became an unavoidable nightly ritual. Michael and I had developed a system of giving each other evenings off. It was my night off, and I sat on that swing, hearing the usual wailing start up, and I almost smiled at the old criticism that it was unfair to give our daughters a peaceful home environment if they could not have that on their own someday.

"Peaceful?" I half-smiled. "You think *this is* a peaceful household?"

*　　*　　*

Nobody dreams of growing up to be the mother who screamed, "Just stop this!" so loudly that she hurt her throat—I mean, genuinely injured it. For two days after. Nobody wants to grow up to be the mother who battled serious depression for a solid year of her children's lives. And as neighbors increasingly looked at us askance, I lost the last of my confidence. Why was I still so often surprised? Why was I unable to anticipate, and to plan a calm reaction to the next violent or destructive act? Why couldn't I control my daughters like other mothers controlled their girls?

Other girls visiting our home after school glowed at me over peanut butter cookies and said their moms were "awesome." I had bite marks from one of my girls, which I hid beneath my sleeves as I smiled and nodded back.

At mothers' meetings, I felt like everyone around me was Carol Brady, but I'd turned into Mrs. Munster. Well meaning, but....

*　　*　　*

There was humor, and there was fun, and there was also Sunday school. We were (and remain) passionately committed to teaching peace and social justice from a Christ-centered perspective, but in our moments of teaching social justice and nonviolence, our little children were on our knees, and we were practicing the restraint holds we were trained in, trying to hold down the level of violence in a child who could not restrain herself on her own—wishing our other two children were not there to stand by and watch.

I can still see Helena at age seven, staring in horror one night while we tried for almost four hours to calm Livia. We could not let go or she would hurt someone. Anyone. Helena had become frozen to the spot. She couldn't look away. She couldn't move.

It was 11:00 p.m.

On a school night.

Beneath the screaming from Livia, I heard a soft, strange, new noise. I looked up at Helena.

She had wet her pants.

I gave her a silent, sympathetic look, but I could not, could not, could not let go of Livia to comfort Helena. Once again I was thinking, "What have we done?"

Then Tim, twelve years old by now, came down the stairs and he was smiling. So amazing. Smiling. I wondered if he had reached his limit. But I quickly understood what he was doing. He strode through the living room with deliberate calm, like he was in some sunlit field. With chaos swirling around the room, Tim had eyes only for Helena. He walked up to her, bent down, took her chin, and forced her to turn her head and look at him. When she did, he smiled at her, and she burst into tears.

It worked. This was the thing that unfroze her.

He lifted her in his arms and carried her outside and down to the wagon in the front yard. At 11:00 at night, my baby was in a safer, more peaceful place outside with her brother pulling her up and down the sidewalk in a red wagon than she was inside my home.

*   *   *

There were plenty of lovely moments in between the chaos—moments that made it all worth it. Early that autumn, the roof cooled off just enough to make it a nice warm place to sneak away to in the early evenings, and I started slipping out the upstairs bathroom window to sit on the roof and pretend to read a book while Michael played basketball with the kids.

But I seldom read. These were the best moments. I could not look away.

Instead, I set down my book to hug my knees, and hidden among the oak leaves I watched my children play.

*   *   *

Miracles happen.

The good news is that they came to us all.

After hospitalizations, and family therapy, and helpful (and not-so-helpful) social workers, both girls grew up to be quite the miracles. Helena will always have FAS, and all the behaviors and all the bad choices that go with the worst of that, but she has managed to find relative happiness in an unortho-dox community of fellow sufferers, whom she treats with the same compassion, patience, and untold generosity I saw Tim lavish on her.

Biggest miracle of all is Livia. Our best family psychologist once told us, "She'll get worse as she goes through adolescence. She's already doing more than normal parents are equipped to or meant to handle. But when she gets through adolescence, you may just get her back. She is a kind soul, and what she needs most is a body big enough to handle the heavy-duty psychotropic drugs she needs now but can't handle. When her body is ready for those, if she will take them, I predict you will get her back."

And he was right.

Livia has become a beautiful, popular, extremely warm and compassionate, bubbly, good-humored young woman to whom others are attracted. The drugs are enormously expen-sive, and she needs quite a few on a daily basis. And they have unpleasant side effects. But once she accepted that these side effects would be a fact of life for her, she embraced the drug regimen, and these medications have allowed the warm, vivacious, real girl—the real Livia she has always been—to emerge. I could not ask for a more amazing, compassionate, joyful daughter.

But what about the issue of race?

Black children in a multi-race family deserve to grow up in a supportive, positive, integrated community. We were lucky. We had that before we had the girls. Not just in our neighborhood and our schools, but we had that in our church and in our choice of close friends. All these great friends did more than keep me from losing it—they also helped all three children grow up to be positively integrated into their own racial communities, while having the bonus of being comfortable in almost any social setting or strata. What people warned was a disadvantage became a boon, a gift, that not all of us possess. But it would not have happened if we had not integrated our lives before we had the children in the first place.

Wait long enough, persevere long enough—ignore the stares and cruel comments long enough—hang in there long enough, and miracles tend to happen.

*   *   *

When you are trying to live what you want to believe in, trying to teach it, trying to give it, you will fall flat on your face, and there will come a time when you are *not* teaching your children. There will come a time when you stumble—and it may be a long fall (like mine was, into fear and depression—and let's not forget the occasional shrieking—that lasted over a year). Or it may be a small fall. But if you are lucky, your children just might take up the cause and teach you.

This last happened to me that night when Tim carried Helena out of the house in his arms. And it happened again the day all three of them taught me to embrace my Mrs. Munster status. It was May, and I was just getting the children ready for school when the hospital called.

"Is this Helena's mother?"

My hands shook and I wished I knew how to smoke, or that I at least owned a baggie of coffee I could inhale. Damn my earth-mother ways.

Our youngest, our Helena, on top of her battles with fetal alcohol, had been having other significant health struggles. Two days before this phone call we had received bad news: Her body had stopped manufacturing its own growth hormone, and injections she'd been receiving were not having any effect on getting it started again. But now there were new test results. The latest batch of blood tests proved her growth hormone had started up again. She had every chance of growing to a normal height!

I hung up the phone and looked at the children, who were spreading a masterfully colorful combination of jams and preserves across a table tiled in toast, in their pajamas. ("Taste Test Time": This was a game we played now and then, with jams this time, but usually with brands of cocoa.) They had stopped the taste test to watch me when I'd answered that phone. They could tell from certain words what this phone call was about.

I looked at my youngest and smiled.

"Helena," I said, taking her face in my hands, "you are going to grow up to be a fine, tall, gorgeous woman. Gorgeous. Tall. *You*," I repeated, my nose nudging hers, a melding of apricot, strawberry, and raspberry jam between us.

The girls laughed and Tim cheered. Old enough to realize Helena's condition had been fairly serious, Tim also had tears in his eyes.

I stood and marveled that here they were: three beautiful children with daily struggles that children in the houses around us never had to deal with. While it felt as if the neighbor children all lived family lives worthy of sitcom charm, mine struggled with behavioral pathologies and the occasional rudimentary criminal elements that no amount of Sunday school and bedtime stories could assuage.

Yet here they were, beaming at each other and at me.

It was a Monday, a school day, but my children were smiling at me and at each other—all three happy about good news for once. That, and it was spring.

"That's it," I said, hands on hips. They set down their (bread) knives expectantly.

"No one in this house is going to school today. We are going on a picnic at the zoo!"

A cacophony of cheers, two tossed napkins, a tossed bowl—full of milk, but oh well—and they scrambled up the stairs to get dressed.

I sat on the couch, tears in my eyes as I lifted my chin to listen: Upstairs, just over my head, my children were all three happy at the same time. *My* children. Just like all those other families that I imagined were so happy—*my* children were accomplishing that, right now, in this moment.

They were going on a picnic in the middle of a school day.

They were going to the zoo.

They were happy.

But this wasn't over.

I was putting the last peanut-butter-and-jelly sandwiches into my backpack, balancing the bananas on top, when the doorbell rang.

Don't answer, a voice in my head said.

I answered. (Idiot!)

It was my classy, gorgeous neighbor, Trudy. She was visibly shaken. I caught her arm.

"Come in!" I gasped. "Are you all right? Sit down."

She sat.

My children started down the stairs, curious, then stopped and lined up to sit on the steps and watch. They stayed where they were. They didn't think she liked them — and she was shaking. They had a right to be wary.

"I have something to tell you," she said. She was very unhappy.

"What is it?" I said. I sat beside her.

Trudy turned to look at me and then said, her voice shaking with anger, "Your cat has left footprints across the roof of my car."

I swear this is true.

I have three witnesses who will back me up.

I stared at her dumbfounded for a moment. Then I glanced out the window where her BMW did indeed have a light dusting of cat tracks across it.

I wasn't sure she was serious.

But should I offer to dust off her car?

Do BMWs need some sort of special cleaning?

I looked then at the children, watching me over the dried-jellied banister.

"What are you going to do about this?" Trudy said, still shaking and livid.

I looked at Livia, the child whose black circles under the eyes always preceded an organically induced long night of raging. Her eyes were clear and light, the eyes of a child excited about the prospect of the zoo and nothing more.

I looked at Helena, the delicate fetal-alcohol victim who today was not a victim at all: She had triumphed over her own body's suppressions and faced, just this minute, the prospect of normal height. She seemed very impressive to me. A dazzle.

I looked at Tim, the oldest, the compassionate, funny, gentle one — the child whose life I was said to have ruined by creating this unique little family. He was supremely happy, his arms around both little sisters. Happy, but slightly puzzled by Trudy.

In fact, I realized something: They all looked wary.

They were far too used to looking wary. To being judged by neighbors. Where were the smiles of a moment ago?

No, I thought. *Don't do this. No, where are your smiles?*

I looked then back at Trudy. I'd almost forgotten she was there. Trudy, in her beautiful clothes, all set for work, and so unhappy. What was she doing here again? What was it she said?

As if she read my mind, she set her delicate jaw and repeated: "What are you going to do about it?"

About what? I wondered, and I was not being sarcastic. I was genuinely trying to remember what the big, serious "it" was all about.

The cat scratched to be let in the front door, and Trudy, her flawless face pinched in utter fury, turned to glare out at her car and its dusty prints.

Oh, I thought. *That.* I remembered.

And then I laughed.

I didn't mean to, but I laughed. It bubbled out of me before I knew it was there.

"Well," I said, standing to let the cat in, "I can push her off next time I see her on your car." I turned to smile at Trudy. "How about that? And I can dust your car off right now, if you like."

My offer was genuine, but I think the fact that I was laughing threw her off. She blinked at me a moment, then stood and left.

The four of us gathered at the window and watched as she drove away. Then the children looked at me and waited, serious-faced.

"Well," I said. "Who wants to see some tigers?"

We all climbed into our beat-up VW van, the one that had plenty of paw prints on the dirty, dusty roof. None of us had said anything. Not a word. I helped the two youngest with their seatbelts, then climbed up into the front seat. Just as I was about to turn the ignition, Tim, my oldest, said, "Mom?"

I looked at him in the rearview mirror. "Mm hmm?"

He was staring at Trudy's empty driveway.

"Tim?"

"Mom, what kind of a life is that to be upset about a cat print?"

I sat back a moment, the keys swinging softly in the ignition, and gazed into the rearview mirror.

I drank in the looks on all three faces. Their looks were befuddled pity.

Okay. You can claim it was just codependence (like when they tell you your baby's smile is really gas), but I saw something else entirely: While I was wondering what I had done to them, my children were thinking their life was better than the life next door with the BMW. They were glad that they knew a cat on a hot ride's roof was nothing to be upset about. Not in the least. There were whole other battles out there more worthy of our attention, and my children, for at least that moment, seemed glad they knew the difference.

Please Don't Shoot Your Mother

Cynthia Yoder

Cynthia Yoder, author and life-purpose coach, is the mother of Gabriel, age thirteen. Returning to her roots during a personal crisis in her twenties led to the publication of *Crazy Quilt: Pieces of a Mennonite Life*, in 2003.

Her writings have appeared in such places as *New Jersey Monthly* and *Mothering*, and she has been noted in such publications as *Glamour*, *Woman's Day*, and *First for Women*.

IN MY NUMBNESS, I glued myself to the television for a few days, hoping to see some order arise out of the chaos. While I was sure to keep the television off when Gabriel, who was then four, was around, it was only a matter of days until what I was protecting him from at home emerged in sandbox chatter at preschool. September 11 hit our country, and life changed. Gabriel now came home talking of bombs and guns, and our peace-loving household had its first internal crisis.

My mind wanted to rewind to only two days earlier, on the morning after the attacks. I woke up feeling the grief of our former city of residence, my face puffy with tears. Gabriel came into the room to make sure I was awake. Seeing my face, he looked perplexed. And then he went into action. He marched back to and from his room three times, returning with his music boxes. He set all of them up on the floor beside me: a clown, a snow globe, a teddy bear. As he sat cross-legged among his treasures, he wound each of them up, making them all go at once. Then he sat there, listening with me. This strange music — which included the teddy bear singing "America the Beautiful" — broke my heart open. It was just the music therapy I needed, brought by hands too innocent to understand.

Now, only two days later, it seemed he'd traded music boxes for bombs.

Gabe and I had a chat.

"You know how it's not nice to hit other kids when you're upset?"

He nodded.

"Well, using bombs and guns hurts people too."

He nodded again, his wide, chocolate-pudding eyes looking so innocent behind his unruly blonde bangs. But the lure of this new realm was not to be undone. On our walks in the woods, Gabriel began looking for sticks shaped like guns. How could I argue with shooting a tree? But then he turned the gun toward me.

It was a new day in America and a new day for this pacifist.

I decided to ask my dad about it. My dad is a longtime Mennonite minister, who — instead of going to the Korean War as a young man — enlisted in Alternative Service, teaching migrant workers in Arizona. Later, as a pastor, he — along with my mother — led youth groups, teaching young people about peaceful solutions to interpersonal and global problems. Both my sister and I grew up with an understanding that peace comes through forgiveness and right relationship, not through war. I was certain my dad would have some kind of solution for me.

"Well, I will tell you what I think, but I don't know that you'll like my answer," he said.

I told him to shoot. Well, no, to go ahead.

He said when he was a young boy, growing up in the rolling hills of eastern Pennsylvania, he and his buddies played "cowboys and Indians" in the woods during lunchtime and recess at school. He told me how they made guns and pistols from sticks and had well-worn trails leading to hideouts and "jails." This, despite the fact that my grandparents held traditional Mennonite views about pacifism. He told me not to worry so much about Gabriel. He said our example as parents and the example of our spiritual community (I was attending a Quaker meeting by then) provided much more instruction than our son would get from any kind of strict rules about gun-play.

"Look at me," he said, with a little grin. "I think I turned out okay."

I couldn't believe my ears. I thought for sure my dad must be a special case, that perhaps he had a special "pacifist" gene. I couldn't imagine allowing Gabriel to run rampant with his war fantasies. And yet, after this window into my dad's childhood, I relaxed a little. I tried to see the situation from my son's point of view. I could see that through his eyes, there was no war. He didn't imagine death and destruction coming from the other end of his finger or twig. He merely saw that he could put his little fingers together like one of his buddies did, and that when he said "bang" his friend acted very silly and fell over onto the floor "dead." He also saw (I am certain) the power behind his gesture as he studied the reaction from the adult world— especially his mother's reaction.

I decided to try my father's advice, and put my worries— and my purism—aside. My husband, Jonathan, agreed with this approach. As the son of Mennonite missionaries, he grew up with so much control around violence and play guns that when he was a teenager, he was fascinated by the whole culture of war. He told me he might have enlisted in the Army had it not been such a taboo in his family.

We decided to allow Gabriel his fantasy play. Since Gabriel has no siblings, I became the favorite target—big, moving, reactive, sometimes feigning a hit. Soon, rules did emerge, out of my need to have space in which I was not turning around to find someone pointing a finger gun or a stick at my face. At first it was: "Gabriel, don't shoot your mother!" Then, after watching him and his friends: "Don't shoot at people's faces!" Then as he grew older and had acquired a realistic-looking plastic gun, it became: "Don't shoot people!" He could aim his plastic gun at targets, or at most, squirrels. I knew this took a lot of the fun out of the game, but Gabriel made up for it in the summer. After a year of his begging, I caved and bought Gabriel the Super Soaker, a water gun that looks like an automatic even Arnold Schwarzenegger might not want to hoist.

Our philosophy, though never written on the wall, is to help Gabriel develop strong inner resources so he can have the strength and tools to choose the way he should go as an adult. We give him direction in how to have peace with himself and his life at home, peace with his peers, and peace with his life at school. While he is not allowed to glut himself with violent input, some is allowed for the sake of keeping up with his friends—and for working out his relationship with this aspect of our culture.

I'm not always comfortable with our choices. My tolerance for screen violence, for example, is just about zero. Watching the entire *Star Wars* series last year together as a family, I groaned out loud during some of the battle scenes, so that both my husband and son told me to be quiet or go find something else to do. And recently, after hearing Gabriel's pleas to let him finish a movie he'd started with a friend, we went so far as to watch *The Matrix*. Though I'd seen the movie before, it was at the very edge of my tolerance level to expose him to so much person-to-person violence. My compromise was that I told him to close his eyes for some parts, even though I know he peeks behind his fingers.

As Gabriel grows into his teenage years, I know the lines we draw may be even more difficult to decide upon. This may be the time that the choices reflected in our community become more important than what my husband and I choose. I treasure our spiritual and neighborhood communities, knowing we are not alone in imparting values of peace and justice and right relationships. Recently, some friends came over to our house to sing peace songs from the 1960s. Our collective group of children joined us for some of the songs. I looked over at the children as they sang, their faces heart-breakingly cherubic: "If I had a hammer…I'd hammer out love between my brothers and my sisters, all over this land…."

Gabriel turns twelve this summer, and by now he has learned about things I wish he would never have to learn about. He has struggled through a book about the Holocaust, and through conversation he has learned how personal the tragedy of 9/11 is to one of his friends who lost an uncle then. I look back at the days of being shot in the derriere with a finger gun as so pure in their innocence. More and more the kind of peace we are imparting to Gabriel is how to create peace within, as his world expands to encompass knowledge of violence going beyond anything he ever encountered in worlds of fantasy.

Gabriel's primary passion is composing songs on the piano. His desire, he says, is to bring joy to people through his music. Those stick-gun-gripping four-year-old fingers are growing and changing, and creating new worlds as they go.

Sometimes, when I really step back from it all, I wonder which one of us teaches the other more about the ways of peace. While I offer Gabriel guidance, he has given me challenges that have made me question what I hold as doctrine and what I hold as truth. And while I offer Gabriel maternal love, his tender heart teaches me how to live peaceably every waking day.

Battle Lines

Jan Pierce

Jan Pierce is a freelance writer living in Vancouver, Washington. She writes devotional material, education-related pieces, and family-life articles. She is a retired teacher, mother of two, and happy grandma to three terrific boys. She has been married for forty-four years and she and her husband spend several months each year doing missions work in India.

Follow her blogs, "One Handful of Rice" (www.onehandfulofrice.org), and "Words for the Journey" (www.janpierce.net).

WHEN I answered the phone that soft spring afternoon and heard my father's voice on the other end of the line, I knew immediately that something was wrong. Sweet, quiet Daddy never made phone calls—he left telephoning to Mom, who had enough words for both of them. My chest tightened as I braced for bad news. My apprehensions were confirmed: My only sibling, my twenty-three-year-old brother, had been wounded in Vietnam. My gifted, Eagle Scout, Army-scholarship brother had been struck down by nine bullets, three of them lodged in his brain. He was alive, barely, and in a coma. He'd been sent to a hospital in Japan after surgery in a field hospital. In spite of all I'd just heard I still hoped Daddy could minimize the damage, change the reality.

"Is it really bad, Daddy?"

"Yes, it's very bad," he said.

The year was 1970, and my husband and I were living in Berkeley, California. I was finishing up a teaching assignment, and we were anticipating the birth of our first child. It was the turbulent, anti-war, grow-your-own years in our part of the United States. High school and college friends were dying in the steamy jungles of Vietnam, unable to identify friend from enemy with any certainty. Fresh-faced graduates one spring, these young men returned in coffins before the next—thousands of them. Back home young people were shocked and sickened at our country's behavior halfway around the world. We protested, we marched, we lobbied, we organized. My opposition to the war was a blow to my parents. My father served all four years of WWII as a medic, earning a bronze star for bravery while my mother waited faithfully for him to come home. I knew how those four years had impacted their lives. The only times I saw my father cry were the rare occasions when he talked about his war experiences. My parents had made life-changing sacrifices during those WWII years, and they couldn't understand how I might question our country's military endeavors to "protect our way of life." I didn't try to convert them to my thinking because I knew their reality and mine were worlds apart. Spring turned to summer and then fall. The news of my brother's condition was sparse. As I tracked the weeks of my pregnancy and the life inside me, I wondered if my baby would ever know his uncle.

I loved my little son, born on a cold December day months after that heart-crushing phone call. I vowed he would never go to war, would never learn violence as a means of solving problems. I would see to that personally with all the maternal ferocity of a lioness—all 110 pounds of me! My firstborn—my heart—and then his sweet little sister, were my life. I poured out myself every day to love, nurture, and train them in the way to walk peacefully in our good world. No toy guns or G.I.

Joe action figures for us. I fought my children's tendencies to turn innocuous wooden blocks into shooters they held in their chubby hands. "No-no, we don't shoot." It did occur to me that little boys need to make noises when they play and that shooting noises were amongst them. Still I persevered in redirecting violent play into nonviolent.

Though my parents were probably unaware, I began to form my pacifist convictions at an early age. I was a quiet child, eager to please. My brother, on the other hand, was high-strung and outspoken. He was challenging to manage and my parents were often pushed to their limits raising him. One day when I was about nine years old my little stinker of a brother teased me once too much. I balled up my fist, pulled back my arm and roundhoused him, my fist landing on his back with a tremendous thud. Immediately I felt sick to my stomach and vowed then and there that my brother could tease me forevermore—he could skin me alive—and I'd never hit back again. I carry the memory of that experience as a marker of the way God has made me to live—without violence, without retribution.

Although my brother always earned excellent grades, he went from crisis to crisis in school. He offended those in authority and struggled to follow rules he didn't respect. But he finally found his niche in programs offering him both acceptance and structure. He entered the Boy Scouts and over a period of years worked his way to the top, thriving in that environment of discipline and accomplishment and becoming an Eagle Scout. In his senior year of high school my brother developed a flag-raising ceremony for our high school, and the summer after his graduation he and three other graduates crisscrossed the United States, demonstrating the ceremony and staying at local Veterans of Foreign Wars (V.F.W.) posts. That same summer he received a full college scholarship from the U.S. Army. He was proud of himself. And my parents, so often at their wit's end in raising him, were proud too.

Now this same little brother lay in a military hospital in a coma, for several months. And then, though no one expected it, my brother awoke. Terribly confused and suffering flashbacks of battle scenes, he was verbally aggressive with both staff and visitors at the hospital he had been transferred to in New Mexico, and he was placed in a psychiatric ward to begin a course of rehabilitation. My parents barely recognized this angry, agitated young man who cursed his way through each day. They were told by doctors that he would regress to the emotional level of a ten-year-old. We all struggled to hold out hope for a full recovery.

As the months passed my brother made some progress both physically and mentally. Brain damage caused him to walk with a limp. He had lost his peripheral vision. And more importantly, he had lost cognitive ability and emotional maturity. Then, inconceivably, less than a year after he woke up, the Army released him from the hospital, promoted him to captain, and discharged him shortly thereafter. The last thing my brother wanted was a discharge; he wanted a lifelong military career. He fought that discharge with everything left in him, but no amount of paperwork, petitions, or recommendations were able to gain him reentry to the military system in which he had invested his brilliance, his promise, and his dreams. In a last-ditch effort to rejoin the military he took up the clarinet he'd played in high school and tried out for the Army band. He was rejected.

*   *   *

By the time my son was five years old we were living in Oregon and had joined the Mennonite Church. I loved the Mennonite teaching on peace and justice. I loved the way men and women chose their careers with an eye to serving humanity. Should war break out, they prepared for alternate service and were willing, if necessary, to serve prison terms rather than engage in military activities they found immoral and in opposition to Christ's teaching. Our fellowship in the Mennonite church helped to solidify peace convictions for my husband and me. In the first few years of our marriage, my husband, who had enlisted in the National Guard and then filed as a conscientious objector, faced the possibility of a jail sentence for non-compliance. We had meetings with a representative of the American Civil Liberties Union; and I was given a little booklet for spouses of inmates, advising me on ways to cope with the years of a sentence meted out for "willing and continual disobedience of orders." It had been a confusing situation for both of us. He had entered the military with the intent of serving the country he loved, but soon realized he was called to a different way — a higher call to honor God over country. He eventually was granted a general discharge as he moved toward a desire to attend seminary and serve God in that capacity. Now our church family helped us put those experiences in perspective, and supported our decision to move toward a life of ministry.

When my son entered third grade we were pleased to enroll him in a Christian school, wanting Christian values to guide his learning. He loved his new teacher who was bright, energetic, and caring, but who was also very supportive of military action. That entire year my son was bombarded with messages about "honor," "patriotism," and "fighting for freedom." *Fighting for Freedom* — he loved those words and the images they conjured up of valiant battles in which good overcame evil. I did my share of re-teaching and un-teaching, but I knew he was in love with the military depiction of courage and the stories of heroes in action. He was learning about the kinds of courage and commitment Christians need to understand, but those lessons came through a military context. How could I guide my son to embrace peaceful ways without confusing him? How could I teach him peace without undermining the authority of his teacher?

I prayed.

I spent a great deal of time in prayer for my brother as well. He remained a shadow of his former self. Broken.

During my son's fourth grade year we lived in Virginia while my husband attended seminary, and we took in all the nearby historical sights, including Jamestown; Monticello; Williamsburg; Washington, D.C.; and Gettysburg.

North vs. South, Abraham Lincoln vs. slavery, good vs. evil, uniforms, soldiers, and battle: My little boy lived and breathed the drama of our nation's most destructive battle, the Civil War. He drew intricate pictures of stone walls and lines of soldiers with their guns and cannons. He spent hours detailing every aspect of the battlefield that was so burned into his imagination. And I let him tape his pictures on the wall because he loved them, while my heart ached with sadness for the dead soldiers—brother fighting against brother.

The years sped by and soon we were in the midst of the activities of junior high and high school. Once again, my son had many teachers who were dyed-in-the-wool military supporters. One very loving and kind principal, an exemplary honorable Christian man, spoke at devotions, and with tears in his eyes he shared how proud he was of one of his graduates who now served our country as a fighter pilot. *Machine guns, bombs, destruction,* and *mayhem:* These words never entered his vocabulary as he praised this young man and his accomplishments. The principal's speech was all about crisp uniforms and salutes and a young man determined to stamp out evil. How could I counteract the words of these Christian role models who taught that fighting was honorable if it was "fighting for freedom," and that killing and carnage were godly if done to an "enemy"? I chose to stand my ground, model a peace-filled life, and love my son, trusting God for the rest.

Parenting is a long process of letting go. As a school teacher I understand the principle of scaffolding, learning by providing a decreasing level of support as a child gains independence. But that principle was difficult to put into practice in my own home. More than once as the time neared for my son to leave home, I thought of baby robins leaving the nest as fledglings. Mother robins stay nearby, watchful, as the baby leaves the nest for the first time. Letting go too early would surely allow a cat to pounce on a baby bird not yet ready to take wing with his own strength. Conversely, hanging on too long would be counterproductive—it would cripple the fledgling's necessary development. I purposely embraced the knowledge that each individual chooses his or her own belief system. My son would soon strike out on his own. He'd go on to college and embark on a career path. I couldn't choose his toys anymore or counter aggressive behavior with re-teaching. He had to make his own choices. I had to pray more and say less.

While my son was growing up and preparing to leave home, my brother had been making an effort to find life after serving in the military. He tried going back to school and failed. He invested in several businesses and lost his money. He finally went to barber school and opened his own shop, where he worked for twenty or more years and then took an early retirement. He was married for a short period of time and then divorced and began living on his own despite his limp and serious vision loss. Because one half of his brain is completely atrophied, V.F.W. doctors track my brother's behavior and abilities, and marvel at his capabilities despite such a serious injury.

My own son will be forty next December. He never joined the military — probably couldn't, we later found out, due to a hearing loss — but he does work for the United States federal government. His job deals with trade and negotiations with foreign countries. He's known for his ability to listen and mediate difficult issues while showing respect for other cultures. He arrived at his own belief system as we all do — by sorting through all he was taught, all he observed, and all that God led him to take into his heart. He's a strong, caring, peaceful adult. I'm very proud of him.

Parenting is risky business. It's an offering poured out continually from the day a child is conceived and forever after. It isn't a perfect offering, but it's the best we have to give as imperfect beings who, like our children, are also learning to walk humbly with our God. There's no guarantee our children will receive the careful training we so diligently work to give, but we make the offering anyway.

My parents did their best for my brother and me. They gave all they had to nurture us and to provide us opportunities they didn't have. My husband and I followed a different path, yet our goals were the same: to give our children the very best we could. And then, we stood back and watched the fledglings take wing.

Hey, Little Kid, Carve that Pumpkin

Polly Rose Peterson

Polly Peterson lives in Dundee, Oregon, with her husband of just more than twenty years and two children—a daughter who is graduating from high school this year and a son who is a sophomore.

In addition to teaching writing at the college level, Polly has also taught high school social studies and preschool. She likes vacationing with her family, both immediate and extended, usually near water—oceans, lakes, rivers, or pools.

"I CAN'T WAIT to get home and carve this pumpkin into a jack-o'-lantern," Bailey says as we drive toward home, having just visited a local farm a few weeks before Halloween. My son Bailey, five, sits in the backseat of our car, next to a Keegan, a classmate from preschool. Bailey and Keegan, and all of the other preschool students, selected a pumpkin as part of the farm tour.

While normally I wouldn't, on this morning I bristle at Bailey mentioning carving a jack-o'-lantern. The celebration of Halloween has become a controversy at the Christian preschool my son attends. Some parents don't celebrate Halloween; some don't see the harm. The teacher had planned a carving party during the school day, but parents complained so she cancelled it, sending the pumpkins home with the students instead.

Keegan's family doesn't celebrate Halloween. We do.

Bailey grows quiet, holding the small pumpkin on his lap. In my rearview mirror, I see him turning it in his hands, picturing the face he is going to carve into it.

"You know who makes you want to do that?" Keegan says. I listen closely. Here it comes, the discussion about Halloween. Bailey doesn't know there is disagreement about Halloween, about jack-o'-lanterns. He only knows it as the day where he carves pumpkins, dresses up, gets lots of candy, and also gets really, really cold walking the streets of Dundee, pelted by Oregon rain.

"You know who makes you want to do that?" Keegan says again.

"Do what?" Bailey asks.

"Carve the pumpkin. You know who makes you want to do that?" Keegan replies.

"No," Bailey answers, a little unsure of where this is going.

"The Devil," Keegan says. "Yeah, the Devil comes up to you and says..." and at this point Keegan changes his voice. He makes it very low, very gruff, and says, *"Hey, little kid... carve that pumpkin!"*

Bailey pauses and thinks about this. Then he answers, "No he doesn't."

"Yes he does," Keegan says with authority. "My parents told me he does that, and my parents know everything."

This is too much for Bailey; exasperated, he calls out to me. He doesn't ask me about the Devil (I don't know if he has ever even heard of the Devil before); he doesn't ask me about whether it is okay to carve pumpkins. No, what he is exasperated about is the statement that parents know everything.

"Mom?" he calls, "Do parents know everything?"

Now, I am into it. I was hoping to avoid a discussion about Halloween with Keegan around. But this question is even more complex than just whether it is right, or not, to wear costumes and trick-or-treat. This question is about truth and how we learn what is true. How do I answer that question? I quickly balance my words. I want to speak honestly to my son, but I don't want to undermine Keegan's beliefs. Undermine Keegan's parents. At four, Keegan has plenty of time to find out his parents don't know everything. So I answer, "Well, I know your dad and I don't know everything." I relax a little, knowing I have answered his question truthfully, simply, without getting into a discussion of epistemology with preschoolers.

I look in the rearview mirror, unable to read the expression on Bailey's face. Keegan smiles smugly and turns towards my son, "Well my parents know everything," he announces.

When we pull up to Keegan's house, his dad comes out to meet us. To be honest, at this point I am a little annoyed. I had tried to preserve the integrity of Keegan's belief in his parents' wisdom, but at the expense of Bailey's perception of his own parents. I wonder if Bailey is sitting there, asking himself how he got stuck with the parents who don't know everything, while clearly other parents know so much more.

I decide to tell Keegan's dad about the conversation. I try to tell myself doing so is only for the sake of truth. But, trust me, I'm sharing for reasons of pride as well.

"So, interesting conversation in the car, today," I tell Joe, Keegan's dad. "Yeah, the boys were talking and Keegan told Bailey that parents know everything." I skip the part about the pumpkin.

Joe laughs. "He did? Well good for him." There is humor in his voice, but I can also detect pride. "That's the way we like it."

Joe turns away and moves off toward the house with Keegan. I get into the car and drive home. Bailey is quiet, and as soon as we pull up to the house, he runs into the kitchen. I help him locate the serrated carving tool from our utensil drawer, and Bailey begins transforming his pumpkin into a jack-o'-lantern. Next, he places into the pumpkin a candle I dig out of the junk drawer and puts his creation on the front porch. Clearly, the warning about the Devil has not affected him. Maybe he has also forgotten about Keegan's suggestion that, as parents, Brent and I are subpar.

A little later, I am in my office, reading e-mail. Bailey comes to the door.

"Mom," he says, "Keegan believes in the Debil." So, I think, he hasn't forgotten. "Who is the Debil?" Bailey asks.

"It's the *Devil*," I correct him, "and he is mentioned in the Bible." I try to tell Bailey, using language and images he can understand but that won't cause him horrific nightmares—that the Devil is portrayed as an entity that causes evil. I start flipping through the Bible, looking for verses I can use.

Bailey stops me. "Okay," he says. "But, he isn't a man who goes around making kids carve pumpkins!" He says it as a statement, not as a question, then walks out of the room, leaving me to contemplate what he had just worked out for himself. What he had learned about truth.

Reflecting, I realize that this isn't the first time he has made his own spiritual leaps. When Bailey was only four, our little Lhasa was run over by the mail truck. At first, Bailey was grateful our dog was still alive. But that evening he came to my bedroom door, his face transformed into a canvas of unwanted emotion: "Is she going to die someday?" he asked. Yes, I tell him. Then, a new realization begins to form, hanging above his head a like a bucket of water perched on a doorframe. With a nudge of understanding, it cascades down upon him. Overtaken by fear, he manages to choke out, "Am I going to die someday?" Yes, I tell him, holding him as closely as he will let me. (Hope, I think; let me speak hope. The hope of Christ.

Hope of love that defeats death.) Do I tell him about heaven? About a happiness beyond? The curtain between life and death was thin and the gulf between what we know and what we believe yawned before us both. I am sure I said something, but my words must have been inadequate in face of this new understanding. Only a psalmist might know what to say.

Now, at fifteen, my son is struggling with real sorrow. This summer, he lost a best friend to a car accident. We got the call at the end of a meal while vacationing with friends at the coast: His good friend had died at Oregon Health & Science University that evening. The driver of the Honda he had been riding in lost control, slamming into an oncoming van. The people in the van were not seriously injured, but the young driver of the Honda was killed instantly, and the passenger, the fifteen-year-old boy who was Bailey's friend, was life-flighted to emergency surgery. He didn't survive.

After hearing the news, Bailey went to a bedroom. The rest of us hovered in the family room, waiting, seeping in sadness. I wondered what Bailey would do with his grief. Would he face this alone?

"We need to get him back home so he can be with his friends, if he wants that," I told my husband. He agreed. So when Bailey did emerge from the bedroom, I offered him a hug, asking him if he wanted to go home, to be with his friends. The relief was obvious. He hadn't thought of that, but it did sound right. I could tell on his face that even in the grip of a sorrow so new, there was something hopeful: friends to be with, friends who understood his pain. I could have predicted that.

One of the blessings in the whole awful event was that faith had been a shared touch-point between the boys. They had bonded through school and summers spent at each other's houses, but also through church camp and youth group. At the candlelight vigil held just twenty-four hours after the accident, the boy's family spoke clearly of their faith in God. It was a connection.

Then something else happened that I didn't foresee: Bailey exhibited willingness to extend himself, to reach out to other teens and even to the boy's family. During the memorial service nearly a week after the boy passed away, the brother told those gathered how Bailey had said the exact words of solace and comfort that he needed to hear. How did Bailey know to do that? He hadn't faced grief like this before. I didn't know, beyond extending comfort and kindness, how to speak into his sadness. As a parent, it is one thing to not know exactly how to talk to your son about the cultural meanings of a holiday such as Halloween; it is quite another to not know how to comfort him in a time of profound grief.

Fortunately, there is a guide out there bigger than our Sunday-morning services, larger than our philosophy books and theological ministrations. I think as parents we worry about whether we are teaching our kids enough, following as closely as we should the Quaker query: "Do you nurture them toward Christian faith and commitment, giving them the Scriptures for their guide?" But, while we need to be there when they ask, and answer their questions with honesty, it is also comforting that we don't have to have all the answers. That we don't know everything. And in spite of that, or more importantly because of that, there is Jesus with us and within us.

Lilies of the Field

"In pure obedience the mind learns contentment."

(John Woolman)

The Economics of Bouncy Balls

Melanie Springer Mock

Melanie Springer Mock has two eight-year-old sons, Benjamin
and Samuel, and two stepchildren, Melissa (30) and Ryan (26).

She is an associate professor at George Fox University and has
written for a number of publications, including *The Chronicle of Higher
Education*, *Adoptive Families*, and *Christian Feminism Today*, among
others. Her book, *Writing Peace: The Unheard Voices of Great War
Mennonite Objectors*, was published in 2002.

Even though her kids stopped naps five years ago, Melanie still takes
one every afternoon, even at her office.

THE FIGHT IGNITES. One minute, my sons are chattering
nonsense in the car's back seat, and the next, I can hear the
thwack of fist against winter coat, then a barrage of retaliatory
hits. Both boys stretch arms across the Subaru, seatbelts restraining them from a full-on war. Before I can even slow the
car to intervene, Benjamin and Samuel are crying, each injured
by flying limbs, jabs to the eye, well-placed kicks.

"What in the world?" I speak into the rearview mirror,
guiding my car to the curb. "What in the heck is going on back
there?" (I may not say *heck*. I don't know.) Turning into the
darkened back seat, I can just barely see my sobbing seven-
year-olds, holding their wounds. Discarded between them is
the subject of their battle: a broken paddle-ball game, sold for
less than a dollar at any discount store.

"*This?*" I scream. With some restraint, of course. "This is what you are fighting over? This is worth hurting your brother?"

Each boy sputters a rationale, tears and slobber blurring their faces. Sam won a paddle game at the elementary school carnival, earlier that very afternoon. But so had Ben. Sam's paddle game broke a short while later, the ball disconnecting from the paddle, making the toy useless. Recognizing the sudden paddle-ball-game inequity, Samuel—like his brother, a tireless crusader for fairness between siblings—took Ben's game and ripped the ball from its string. Justice has been restored, at least in Samuel's mind: Both boys have the same thing, a broken game. Benjamin, of course, has a different understanding of justice—at least in this instance.

"It's not fair!" Samuel sobs, still smarting from his brother's punches.

"It's not fair!" Benjamin cries, upset by his brother's destruction.

And I want to wail, too: *It's Not Fair*. Because my peaceful ride in the car has been lost to an argument over a stupid, cheap toy. Because my boys are fighting over something so silly. Because I would never, ever, be able to convince them that this life—the life they lead—is more fair to them than they could ever imagine.

I want to wail, too, but I don't.

*   *   *

Long before I have children of my own, my sister calls to complain about her kids—or, at least, about their latest Happy Meal prizes. A few hours post-McDonald's, the Happy Meal-filled children are no longer happy. My niece and nephew, probably about six and four at the time, fight over their toys, neither of them satisfied with whatever Ronald has tossed into their meal bags along with the fries and nuggets. Plus, the toys play an annoying tinny song, eternally stuck in a maddening loop. The arguing, the music, the late-afternoon chaos: all of it somehow makes my sister snap.

"I couldn't help it," she admits to me over the phone. "I took their toys into the garage, and smashed them to bits with a hammer."

I offer her the bemused laugh of a woman without children, of someone who has never confronted the tyranny of Happy Meals toys or the agony of kids arguing over molded plastic junk. But while she continues to unwind her story of temporary insanity, I think to myself, *Wow, my sister is nuts. There's no way I'd ever go crazy over a toy.* I wonder if I should tell her she is making too much of nothing.

For obvious reasons, I don't.

*   *   *

Every year, our small town of Dundee, Oregon, holds several kids-oriented events, including the elementary school carnival, at which my boys win their soon-broken paddle-ball toys; and a fall festival, where neighbors gather to celebrate our community. At both events, kids can play any number of carnival games, for free, and are given prizes at each gaming booth. Awards never seem based on actually winning a game: A kid could wildly miss making a free throw, or could toss a dart far off the balloon mark, and still be given opportunity to choose his or her prize. (Never mind the lesson this teaches children: Go ahead and fail! You will be rewarded no matter the quality of your effort!)

At these events, children are offered either candy or cheap plastic toys from overseas businesses that excel in creating children's ephemera: bouncy balls, finger rockets, temporary tattoos, plastic rings and bracelets. And while I know the event organizers are giving parents a choice between unhealthy prizes, like candy, and the other stuff, I beg my children to take the sugar. As they rifle through a bucket full of temporary tattoos, I plead, voice locked in a sincere plaintiff cry: "Please, have some candy instead. You like Tootsie Rolls, right? Look, there's some Smarties! And a sucker! Anything but the finger rocket."

What kind of parent goads her children into taking more candy?

The kids rarely listen to me, at any rate, and by the time we've left the carnival, both boys have bags stuffed with worthless toys and one or two Tootsie Rolls. At home, they dump their loot on the kitchen table, rub a few temporary tattoos on to their faces (of course!), put on some of their new rings and bracelets, then leave the detritus from their outing—the toys no longer appealing, or already broken—scattered all over the table top. Within hours, I will find plastic rings on the floor; finger rockets shot into our house plants; bouncy balls, half chewed by our dog, in the corners of rooms.

As I walk through the house, picking up junk, surreptitiously throwing stuff away, already cursing our afternoon at the carnival, my blood boils. Like my sister, pounding cheap toys into her garage floor, I seethe with righteous anger, swiping up toys and railing—silently, at least—about the stupidity of it all. Why do we have these carnivals? Why do event organizers think kids need all this junk, cheap and easily broken, dumped into landfills within hours of being "won"?

My own anger seems fueled by the larger issue these crappy toys represent. It's hard for me to teach my kids economic justice when they are treated to material goods each time they attend a school carnival or purchase a kids' meal or even say a Bible verse at church; when they are rewarded for doing nothing much; when the toys themselves show me how much they have, especially compared to the children whose parents probably made the very items we so easily discard.

I vow that at the next carnival, I will demand my kids not take any toys at all, that they will win candy or nothing whatsoever. I make my silent pledge, but at the next kids' event where cheap toys are de rigueur, I don't keep it.

Of course I don't.

*   *   *

It happens about once every month: I succumb to buying my kids a fast-food kids' meal. Usually, I do this because I'm harried, driving them from one son's baseball game to another's soccer match. Or because I realize the food is cheaper, and more plentiful, than anything I could buy from the restaurant's regular menu. Or because my defenses are weak, and I've decided the fight over Happy Meals is not one I'm willing to wage from my car's front seat.

I rarely regret my decision until the boys have finished their fries and Cokes, and are digging in to the kids'-meal prizes that always accompany their orders. When I'm unwrapping layer upon layer of plastic to reveal a trinket that does little except shill for the latest television show or movie, I feel my rage building, again. *Why do I let myself buy this stuff?* I wonder.

And then, I think about people in the majority world when I'm handing my kid a plastic Spongebob that shoots discs from his slotted hands; or a Spiderman figure that moves his arms up and down; or a wind-up R2-D2 that gurgles something unintelligible. I imagine a Chinese worker, shoving these toys into plastic, bemused by the kind of junk that appeals to American materialists. I imagine a child worker in Vietnam, screwing Spiderman's arms to his torso, for hours and hours every day. I imagine someone in India, designing the R2-D2 doll my sons will wind up half a dozen times before its inane garble fails to keep their interests.

I'm tempted to tell my boys about the people who make their kids'-meal toys and the junk they readily win at carnivals and just as easily discard. When they fight over a paddle-ball game, or discard cheap plastic toys into all the corners of our house, I long to give them intricate lectures about economics, about the injustices of sweat shop labor, about the children their age who may be working in factories, creating toys so their families can live. I want to talk with them about the poverty in other nations, and the ways our own country's wealth has contributed to the destitution of others. I want to tell them about what I think Jesus himself would say about economic injustices.

But for some reason, I don't.

*   *   *

We are in India, traveling to the Himalayas for my stepdaughter Melissa's wedding. Before striking off into the mountains to meet our new in-laws, my husband, my boys, and I spend some time in New Delhi as tourists, driving through the crowded city streets in a comfortable air-conditioned car. Even though we've only been in India for twenty-four hours, my boys already appear overloaded by what they see, taste, smell. The hotel's breakfast is too spicy for them, the yogurt too tart. The Delhi smell of dampness and trash and incense overwhelms. The appearance of families sleeping on sidewalks, cattle wandering nearby, green and yellow tuck-tucks weaving through traffic: It all overwhelms, and the boys sit close to me in the car's backseat, unfettered by restraints or seat belts, another sensory change from their normal lives.

At each stoplight, our car is accosted by young beggars, children my sons' age, wearing dirty, too-small clothes. Many of them hold out goods for sale, the same kind of cheap toys my kids win at the Dundee carnival. The beggars tap on our closed windows, holding up their wares so we might see. Because we are easily identified as Westerners, and therefore wealthy, even more children rush to our car. They yell into our closed space, pleading with us to accept their superior products, letting us know they are hungry by holding their clearly bloated stomachs, or by putting their hand to their mouths, communicating that they will buy food with the money we give them.

I've read enough about India to understand begging collectives. I know that many, if not most, of these children work not for their own food, but for gang leaders who confiscate their meager profits in exchange for inadequate meals and, perhaps, a place to safely sleep. Child beggars sometimes learn how to evoke sympathy through feigned illness or, in some cases, through disability forced on them by the criminals for whom they work. Giving the beggars a few rupees — or, even, buying what they sell — only perpetuates an evil system, one that essentially enslaves children.

And so, at the New Delhi stoplights, we remain silent. We stare straight ahead, refusing to acknowledge the poor children knocking at our window. Or, I should say, my husband and I refuse to acknowledge. My boys are intrigued.

"Mom! Look! That boy has Hello Kitty pencils. Can we buy one?" Benjamin asks.

"Why are they selling this stuff here?" Samuel wonders aloud. "Why can't Indians just go to a store?"

"Mom! Look! Can we buy that balloon?" they plead, in unison.

I tell them no, we will not be giving money to the beggars. I even try to explain why: that the children work for grown-ups who force them to sell these toys. Helping my then-kindergarten-aged boys understand an unjust problem perpetuated by poverty is exceedingly difficult. And the image of beggar children does something to my sons too. They seem more subdued as we continue our trip through New Delhi. During the rest of our travels in India, they will ask about the children, and about the toys they are selling, often at inexplicable times: at breakfast, or right before bed, or as we are walking through the Himalayan woods. Their questions suggest to me they are trying, again and again, to get their heads around a situation they may never fully understand: that some children are so poor they lack a home or food; that some children do not go to school, but spend their days begging, forced there by grown-ups; that some children do not play with the toys they sell street-side.

This seems like the perfect opening, the opportunity to lecture them about economic justice. Far away from home, in a country overwhelmed by poverty, I could explain how much better off we are as middle-class Westerners. As my boys wonder about the children knocking at the car window, I could easily talk about how Jesus demands we give up all we own to care for the poor, and that I think our desire to have more stuff probably makes Jesus sad.

I could say these things while we're in India, but I don't.

*   *   *

How do I keep my boys from feeling guilty for the lives they've been given, even as I hope they seek justice for others who have not been so similarly blessed? I want that to be the question at the heart of bouncy-ball economics, and maybe it is: My despair about the junky toys they receive at every turn — and the global inequities those toys represent to me — is countered by a desire to let my kids be kids, shooting finger rockets at each other without fretting about the exploited workers who made them.

To be honest, though, my kids' lust for cheap goods pricks my anger precisely because of my own problematic relationship with materialism. I imagine I could hold tight to my impotent rage, railing at my kids about those exploited workers, about the begging collectives in India, about the oppression wrought by Happy Meals toys. I suppose I might dismantle my kids' sense that life is unfair when their paddle games break by reminding them of the children in India, holding dirty hands to our windows. I could smash all their cheap carnival-won toys to smithereens (oh, believe me, I could!). Yet when I'm tossing half-chewed bouncy balls into the trash, I sometimes remind myself of this: that, as an adult, I also struggle to navigate the challenges of materialism. Living simply isn't so easy, especially when your culture lures you into believing you will be more content with fashionable clothes, or a well-designed kitchen, or a sweet-looking car. Or a temporary tattoo, for that matter.

I would like to say my husband and I model economic justice for our children, showing them how to live simply out of care for the world's poor. But I have the same fascination with shiny things that they have, though on a much larger scale: I don't want finger rockets, but I'd love a new Subaru Forester; I'm not partial to plastic bracelets, but would like to wear a North Face jacket. I find it's hard to teach my children economic justice and simplicity when I purchase clothes, jewelry, cars, household goods, without much — if any — regard for where they were made, and without much thought for how my own materialism further divides a world into "haves" and "have nots."

If anything, then, my boys' own lust for cheap toys reflects my failure to live simply, as well as my own rampant materialism, my lack of consideration for the poor, perhaps my own sense of entitlement about the things I own. And so, if I'm to take bouncy-ball economics seriously, I will first need to accept Jesus' message in the Gospels, and will need to acknowledge what Jesus means when he says if we are to follow him, we must sell everything we have and give the proceeds to the poor (Luke 12).

Everything? I ask, fists curling around my stuff. Surely not.

Oh, certainly I try to justify my own economic choices, try to convince myself we are doing what Jesus says: We drive old cars, wear inexpensive clothes and cheap jewelry, have a house that is in need of updating and remodeling. We give to charities, avoid lavish vacations, use the *More With Less* cookbook, for goodness' sake. But if I am honest with myself, I am just as much a consumer — and, by extension, a potential oppressor of the poor — as anyone else who has rejected the idea that when Christ means we should sell everything, he really means everything.

As my kids grow older (and as I also grow older) we are learning — little by little — what economic injustice looks like, and as a family, we have made some efforts to live by Christ's call to simplicity. Still, more often than not, we fail that call. But we muddle forward, slapping temporary tattoos to our faces and throwing bouncy balls against living room walls — before the dog swallows them, of course. We journey on, hoping that some day, Benjamin and Samuel will learn what living simply — and caring for the poor — truly means. And, hopefully, some day I will learn as well.

Because I really want to live in a world that is economically just. But I don't.

Wealth Isn't in the Crayons

Dorcas Smucker

Dorcas Smucker lives in a ninety-nine-year-old farmhouse in Harrisburg, Oregon, with her husband, Paul, and their six children.

She is a columnist for the Eugene, Oregon, *Register-Guard* and has written three books. She keeps busy with her family, her Mennonite church, writing, sewing, and the family's grass-seed business.

You can read more about Dorcas on her blog, "Life in the Shoe" (dorcassmucker.blogspot.com).

EVEN NOW, I am not quite sure why I bought it. I was at Costco a few weeks ago, scanning the office supplies, and there it was, a thick box of sixty-four Crayola crayons, with the familiar green and yellow lines slanting down the front.

Perhaps I was simply falling for a clever marketing ploy, but those crayons called to me from thirty-five years ago, when to own such a box would have meant that God was smiling on me, life was saying, "Yes!" and all the doors were opening at last.

So I bought it, and it sits on my desk. The top bends back to reveal tiers of pointed crayons in four neat sections. Wild strawberry, turquoise blue, cerulean, chestnut, and carnation pink. I check and yes, they still make crayons in both green-yellow and yellow-green. It even has that cool little sharpener tucked in the back to keep the crayons perpetually new.

I never had a box of sixty-four crayons when I was a child. Twelve or twenty-four, maybe, but never a glorious box of sixty-four like Rachel and Lydia, the two whiny sisters at our little Amish school who did their best to make life miserable for my sister and me. Rachel and Lydia formed "secret" clubs that we were not allowed to join. They hid straight pins in the rest-room towels and waited for us to poke our hands. Worse, Rachel and Lydia were rich. They actually got new shoes in the middle of the school year. I, on the other hand, wore out my shoes and socks until I sometimes went to school with my big toes exposed. They had pretty notebooks and freely scribbled on a paper, tore it out, and then threw it away — an unthinkable waste.

And they had those big boxes of crayons, a luxury that explained their mysterious powers over us, their ability to make us do whatever they wanted even though we resented and even hated them — though we would never have admitted it.

While the Amish are applauded for their sense of community, in some ways they are fiercely independent. To be known as a "poor manager" or to be unable to take care of your family is considered shameful and embarrassing. So my dad, undeniably a "poor manager," taught school for a tiny salary and tried to farm in his spare time, and we were quietly poor. More a scholar than a farmer, Dad bought old, cheap machinery that he didn't know how to fix and farmed with noble but pathetically outdated methods.

Poverty defined our status in the community, our value, and our outlook on life. A black cloud called "the Debt" hung over us, bringing a vague fear of disaster and making us feel that no opportunity would ever knock at our door. Mom filled us up with rice and gravy, vegetables from the garden, chickens that we raised and butchered, and homemade bread. I wore hand-me-down clothes and never had a new coat from a store until I was nineteen and on my own.

Much later, I came to realize that poverty and wealth have as much to do with attitudes, comparisons, skills, resources, and a sense of control over one's life as they do with actual dollars or an arbitrary federal poverty level. "Not having money," my brother, Fred, tells me, "is a symptom of being poor. To be poor is to be caught in a cycle of futility, like going the wrong way on the moving walkway at the airport. Everything works against you, interest on loans piles up, you always choose the wrong things to invest in. To not be poor is to go with the walkway. Even if you sit on your suitcase, you're still moving forward."

To Dad's dismay, my sister and I fantasized about marrying rich men, such as Prince Charles. I did not marry a rich man, and Paul and I refer to the first thirteen years of our marriage as our "poor days." But it was a much different sort of poverty than I had known as a child. Paul had a head for business, and his clearly defined budget of our meager monthly income gave me security and a sense of control. Life could say "yes" even if we were poor, he insisted. When I needed a serger sewing machine, he figured out how to save a little bit each month until we could afford it.

When we lived in Canada on a voluntary-worker stipend, we ate moose meat and rice rather than convenience foods or fresh fruit, and celebrated the children's birthdays with homemade cake and huge soap bubbles blown through bent hangers. When Matt, our son, was in the bandage-every-bump stage, his only gift for his fifth birthday was a box of Band-Aids. I still think he had more fun taping Band-Aids all over himself then he would have had with a $30 remote-control car.

We could never buy much, but with housing provided for us and with Canada's national health plan, we were spared a sense of impending disaster.

The hardest of our poor days was when we came back to the United States after eight years in Canada. Instead of living among equally poor missionaries or the Ojibway, we were surrounded by an intimidating high standard of living. Our children were invited to birthday parties, and we couldn't afford gifts. A church-dinner organizer would hand me a dessert recipe and ask me to make and bring it. Rather than admit I couldn't afford it, I blew the grocery budget on Cool Whip, Oreos, and fudge sauce.

One of the few things I miss about those days is the thrill of finding a great bargain, but mostly, I am not nostalgic about poverty. Grocery shopping was an agony of decisions, coupons, and calculations. Twice, medical emergencies swallowed all our savings.

Sometimes, however, I talk to struggling single mothers and realize how wealthy I was in other ways. Thanks to my mom, I had the skills to use cloth diapers, grow and freeze vegetables, and make clothes and food from virtually nothing. Thanks to my constantly employed husband, I had the time.

Our fortunes began to change when we bought a grass-seed warehouse business from Paul's dad. Today, if I need to, I can walk to Payless ShoeSource and buy new shoes for the children. However, since habits from poor days die hard, I bought all their school shoes secondhand this year. Since we remember what it was like, we try to share with others in need.

In spite of our struggles, we have one shining success from our poor days: Our children say they didn't feel poor. When they reminisce about those years, they don't recall deprivation and garage-sale gifts, but rather going on walks, playing by the lake in Canada, and hunting for tadpoles in ditches here in Oregon. Life, they say, felt full of opportunity.

There is one exception to this: Emily, sixteen, says she will someday bring up in therapy how badly she wanted an American Girl doll, and we never bought her one. I imagine her therapist will tell her that now that she is successful and wealthy, she should simply go buy one to heal the wounds of the past.

And Emily will find that it wasn't about dolls at all, just as I found out it wasn't about having sixty-four crayons. It's about accepting what happened to you, being grateful for the skills and lessons you would not have learned otherwise, and sharing with others. Mostly, it's about forgiving yourself for ever letting Rachel, Lydia, and a box of crayons determine who you were and what you were worth.

Bad Guys

Heidi Cox

Heidi Cox and her husband are the parents of Gabriel (3½), Ezra (2), and a baby girl on the way. Heidi is constantly amazed by how little sleep it takes to actually survive a day. Consuming way too much coffee and writing about motherhood adventures are two of her favorite pastimes. Her sons have taught her more about construction machines, locomotives, and God's grace than she ever imagined possible.

GABRIEL SLID DOWN the park slide with all the gusto a toddler boy was capable of exerting. He smiled at me, waiting for a word of affirmation, and then ran around to the side of the play structure to attempt the mini rock wall. He had limited success, but that didn't bother him. Ducking underneath the slide, he pretended to serve me food made out of bark dust. I watched him, with my proud mommy heart beating loudly. Here he was, my sweet little boy, enjoying the simple things, interacting and helping his younger brother, Ezra — totally content in the moment. Just being himself. Being happy.

Then it happened. A group of older boys descended on the playground. They had their Star Wars light sabers, and they ran around with verve, mock fighting to defeat the dark side. Or so I thought. Until I heard one of them yell, "Okay, now *I'm* the bad guy," with a playful edge to his smile.

"No, *I'm* the bad guy!" another one replied.

"No, me!" called his friend.

And it went back and forth as they vied for the thrill of playing Darth Vader.

Gabriel stopped playing. He stood still, his little head tilted up as he watched in wide-eyed wonder at these six- and seven-year-old boys. He stopped tromping up the slide, stopped making me "food," stopped saying, "Mama, watch this!" Attention from his mommy wasn't nearly as important now as attention from these new kids. He began sauntering around after these "cool" boys, a half-smile on his face, observing their imaginary play and probably hoping they would somehow include him in their game. They didn't pay him any attention, but that didn't deter him. The rest of our time at the park he spent tagging along after these kids.

Later that same day, after his nap, we were standing in the kitchen and Gabriel looked up at me. "Mama, I'm the bad guy!" he said with delight.

I smiled. "Oh, okay Gabriel," I said nonchalantly. But inwardly I was having a slight panic attack. He was still thinking about those boys, wanting to be like them. I know he didn't understand what a bad guy was. But that didn't matter. He wanted to be like those older kids. If they wanted to be bad, he wanted to be bad.

The conversation unsettled me, made me think about how easily Gabriel forgot what was in front of him and was drawn to something that seemed cooler or better. How quickly Mama and the playground faded in importance when something more enticing—older kids, light sabers, bad guys—came along. *Does it really start this young?* I thought, this lure of wanting to be something we're not, to have something we don't? How easily we forget the gifts we have right in front of us. It's our nature. It's my nature.

I smile when I think of how proud my husband, Brian, and I felt after we finished our family goals during our honeymoon. There we were in Kauai, sitting on the veranda of our hotel room overlooking the vast ocean. Our feet were up, our sunglasses on, and we had coffees in hand. We talked, laughed, and dreamed about our future together. Brian and I didn't have children yet, but we wanted to have an idea of where we would head with them, and what kind of values we hoped to instill in our home. It was easy to come up with a list that we both agreed on. When we came home, we displayed the goals in a frame next to our bed. It's a short list, but one of the lines says, "Teach our children the value of contentment."

Contentment, to my husband and me, means enjoying the simple things—being outdoors as much as possible, limiting technology in our home, investing in face-to-face relationships, but most of all we long to be at peace with where we're at, choosing to make the most of what we have, and practicing delayed gratification: being thankful for the gifts God gives us each day, instead of striving for something beyond our reach.

Looking back, it was easy to think about teaching contentment when I was feeling content. I was married to my best friend; we were imagining the adventures that were before us, and setting lofty goals for ourselves and our future children. Through the lens of our honeymoon, what lay beyond the horizon looked pretty rosy indeed.

Fast forward six years.

I trudged through the hallway with pajamas in one hand and diapers in another. I tried to ignore the dirty clothes scattered throughout my path, but it was nearly impossible. I kicked them to the side with an exasperated sigh. Turning into the living room, I realized that Gabriel hadn't gotten far with cleaning up his toys. It looked like a bomb had exploded, with the blast's aftermath—dinosaurs, trucks, Legos, and crayons—scattered everywhere. And then the kitchen appeared in my periphery, full of dirty high chairs, messy tables, and piles of dishes. My one-year-old, Ezra, was pulling at my leg to hold him while two-and-a-half-year-old Gabriel was whining for his pacifier. Brian wouldn't be home for hours yet, meaning I was left to my own devices as I juggled the boys' bedtime routines. Again. We were in the second year of Brian's six-year medical residency. He was gone more than eighty hours a week while I kept the home fires burning—or at least tried to keep the boys from burning down the home.

Oh, how I wished life were different. I wished in my weariness that I didn't have to clean up and pick up and tidy up and put away and bend over to wipe up messes off the floor, off hands, off faces, off bodies. Wishing my husband was home more, wishing I had a maid, or a cook. Wishing, at the very least, that some kind soul would show up at my door with a caramel latte. Was that really too much to ask?

I couldn't remember what a day felt like without my child-rearing responsibilities. I also was having a hard time remembering the last time my husband and I had that blissful feeling we had in Kauai. At this point I had all but forgotten about our list of goals. I was in survival mode, trying to keep my head above water, and trying not to blame everyone else for my agony. My approach wasn't working. I felt sorry for myself and wanted an escape. But there was nowhere to go.

Of course, I love my boys with a love that only another mother can understand—a desperately aching love that longs to keep the good in and the bad out. A love that's willing to do anything for their safety, their happiness, their understanding of who God is and how much God loves them. But even with this deep love, I wanted my children on my terms, not on theirs. I wanted them when they were happy and not fussy. When they were sleeping and not up all night. When they didn't follow me everywhere, including the bathroom. When they had long naps. When they let me cook in peace. When they obeyed every time, the first time. When they played together in harmony for more than thirty seconds. I wanted the fun, clean, restful parts of motherhood—without the messy, frustrating, lonely parts. I wanted the honeymoon to last, not just with my husband, but with my kids. With my life.

Ultimately, deep down, I wanted my life to be like the life of our friendly neighbors across the street. All too often I found myself staring out the window at their house, secretly coveting their lifestyle. They seemed to have everything I didn't. The wife had a housekeeper who came every other week. She had two children spread four years apart: a three-year-old and a seven-year-old. She conveniently had a Starbucks coffee in hand or was on the way to get one most times I saw her. Her husband left for work at 8:30 and came home at 4:30. He was home on the weekends. They were active and social, having people over for get-togethers, going to parties to celebrate birthdays, holidays, Fourth of July, Labor Day—all the three-day weekends my husband didn't have off. *Wouldn't that be nice?* I'd often muse. (My social life consisted of exciting events like standing in line for three hours to get our swine flu shots. While everyone else was complaining about standing in the rain, I was actually relieved to have a reason to get out of my house!)

So here I was, wanting my children to be thankful, to have happy hearts, to be grateful for the gifts God has given them. But I wasn't modeling that at all. I wasn't grateful: I was bitter. I wasn't thankful: I was envious. I wasn't happy: I was resentful. As I gazed at my neighbor's house, I was acting just like Gabriel did with those older boys—chasing after something I didn't have and forgetting what was right in front of me. With a huge plank in my own eye, I was the most discontent of all.

Then one night I was rocking Ezra to sleep. Usually when I rock him I'm making my mental list of what I need to do between the time that he falls asleep and I can go to bed: clean up living room, do dishes, fold laundry, catch up on a few e-mails, then collapse into bed, hoping to get some decent sleep before Ezra would rouse me again at 4:30 with his morning screaming ritual. The goal was to get him asleep fast and get on with my tasks.

But for whatever reason, on this night I looked down at his little face in my arms, and I lingered. He was not terrorizing his brother, or screaming at me, or throwing his food on the ground. He was so—content. His sleeping presence drew me in. I looked at this little person I held and thought, *I won't be rocking him to sleep much longer.*

As obvious as it may seem, it was profound for me to realize that my children are not meant to be held forever. They are meant to be held with a love that slowly releases its grip, year by year, in a way that's almost imperceptible, until I see that I'm not holding them at all. I'm holding onto the memories. And I realized that, when it comes to that point, I don't want to regret that I didn't enjoy the gift of my family.

As I sat in that dark room with my little boy, his steady breathing calming me, his warm body soothing my tension, I thought of all the things I resented, and I began seeing them in a different light. It was like God was birthing a new set of eyes in my heart, and giving me another chance to embrace my life. The lesson was crystal clear: start with my own heart first. As happens often, my children became my teacher.

When I slow down and look at the world from my sons' eyes and at their pace, I see how they intrinsically take joy in the simple things—a bumblebee buzzing around flowers, an ant crawling through the cracks on the sidewalk, the clouds moving across the sky, a robin perched on a tree, a hummingbird fluttering outside our kitchen window, the squirmy worms that are found with delight under rocks.

When I'm content, I can also receive the tender moments of the day, without disengaging myself from them: Ezra blowing me a kiss. Gabriel belting out his Sunday school songs—totally off tune and hilarious. Ezra following his big brother around the yard, mimicking everything he does. Gabriel running to bring a toy to Ezra when he's crying and pushing his little brother on the tire swing. The way Gabriel chimed in during our prayer the other night at dinnertime, "And thank you God, that we found that Thomas the Train backpack at the garage sale. That was really special!" And the way the boys kiss each other goodnight. Discontentment is a thief. It robs me and my family. It steals away the beauty in the moments I am trying to rush by.

I'd love to say I've chosen contentment every time since my epiphany, but I most certainly haven't. I still can't believe how often I'm bemoaning my life. The lure of the "bad guy" seems to lurk around every corner of my mind, begging me to complain and whine and wonder how much fun the neighbors are having. Learning contentment is slow, hard work. It's a long, painful process of God's pruning and refinement. But it's a start. And each day is another opportunity to thank God for it all—the quiet and loud, the messy and clean, the hugs and the tantrums.

The honeymoon is long gone, and that's okay. It's not meant to last more than a short season. Otherwise, I would never understand what it means to live beyond myself, beyond my own gratification, my own needs, my own schedule. I would never grasp the beauty of sacrifice. I would never understand that God calls me to choose contentment because it's the only way to look back on my life with peace.

Buying the Whole Farm

Marta Oti Sears

Marta Oti Sears lives in Sherwood, Oregon, with her husband, Andy, and is the mother of two, Gabriela (9) and Jonah (6). She is also a justice advocate for International Justice Mission. Now that both of her children are in school all day, she hopes to spend more time writing, reading, and having uninterrupted conversations with grown-ups.

MY SEVEN-YEAR-OLD daughter jumped into the van with what looked like a magazine in her hand. "Mom, I have something I really want to do, but I really need you not to say 'no' right away. Well, I don't want you to say 'no' later either. I just *really* need you not to say anything about why you think it might not work, okay?"

This is gonna be interesting, I thought. It was mid-October of Gabriela's second-grade year and, to my knowledge, this was the first time she'd felt the need to coach me on my response to her.

"Okay," I said. "Go ahead."

"You know how the past two Christmases Jonah and I have done extra chores to earn money so we could buy a farm animal from World Vision as our Christmas gift to Jesus?"

"Yes."

"Well, how many chores would I have to do to earn two thousand dollars?"

"Uh…a lot," I replied as the beginnings of a knot started to form in my stomach.

"In library today, Mrs. Richen showed us the World Vision catalog and said that we could tell our parents or grandparents that we'd like to get one less gift this Christmas so that the money that would have been spent on that gift could buy some chickens or a goat for a poor family in another country. But since we've already done that for a couple of years, I want to do something bigger. I want to buy a whole farm! It's right here on page three for two thousand dollars."

I'd like to be able to say that at this point I prayed a silent prayer of praise to God for forming such a beautiful, compassionate heart in my daughter. But truthfully I found myself saying a whispered expletive. Thankfully, since the rearview mirror only exposes my face from mid nose up, she couldn't read my lips or the panicked expression on my face.

I embarked on an internal dialogue-slash-argument with myself.

"Don't squelch her vision!"

"But we don't have two thousand dollars to give away!"

"Actually, we have more than that in our savings account."

"But that's a lot of money! We're going to have to talk her down to a more realistic amount."

"But it's awesome that she wants to be so generous!"

"Is God trying to tell us through our seven-year-old that we aren't generous enough? I thought we *were* generous!"

What I managed to say out loud was, "This is a really big idea. Right now I'm not sure how it could work, but let's talk about it at dinner with Dad."

*　　*　　*

My husband and I have been deeply impacted by a human rights organization called International Justice Mission (IJM). When we first learned about the horrific reality of child sex trafficking, we searched the Internet for a Christian nonprofit that was doing something to help these exploited children, and we discovered IJM. The mission and work of IJM is to rescue and secure justice for victims of slavery, sex trafficking, and other forms of violent oppression. Gary Haugen, IJM's president, has become one of my heroes. I've read all of his books and have heard him on several occasions. At one of his speaking engagements, Haugen told a story that has stuck with me.

Jesus and his disciples were returning from various towns and cities where they had been preaching, healing, and interacting with hoards of people. They had focused on the needs of others for days on end. Now they were tired, hungry, and ready for some peace and quiet.

Just as the disciples were thinking they were about to get some well-deserved time with Jesus, a huge crowd of people showed up. In typical form, Jesus had compassion on the newcomers, and even though he was tired and ready to relax, he chose to spend time talking with them. After awhile, the disciples' patience ran out, and they asked Jesus to send the crowd home. It *was* dinner time after all, and part of caring for people is ensuring that they get proper nourishment at the appropriate times. But instead of dismissing the crowd, Jesus threw his disciples a curveball. "Why don't you feed them?" he asked.

The disciples probably got a little grouchy with Jesus at this point. "Oh sure, Jesus. That would be really fun, and, we might add, a great way to spend the money *we don't have!*" I suppose it's possible they worked out a polite, "That's a good idea, Jesus, but unfortunately we don't have the funds to execute this plan. So what's plan B?" Instead of giving away the solution, Jesus asked another question. "What *do* you have?"

So the disciples scouted out the crowd and came back to report that the only food they could find was a young boy's sack lunch of five loaves and two fish. Jesus asked them to bring it to him. "In that moment," Haugen said, "Jesus took responsibility for the miracle." Jesus prayed and then proceeded to multiply that little boy's lunch enough to feed more than five thousand people, with a boatload of leftovers to spare. "The boy was responsible for obedience," Haugen said, "simply offering what he had so that Jesus could do the miracle."

Haugen pointed out that we, like the disciples, often feel overwhelmed by the immensity of problems like AIDS, hunger, sex trafficking, and natural disasters. Because we realize our resources aren't enough to do everything needed to bring an end to the suffering, we often do nothing. But God doesn't ask or expect us to do everything. "The God of justice is waiting to do miracles," Haugen said, "if we will just offer up our little measure of obedience."

*   *   *

On the day Gabriela dropped the farm bombshell, I snuck in a pre-dinner brainstorming session with my husband, Andy. He marveled at our little girl's big vision while I fretted over the predicament that her precious vision was putting us in. You see, I'm a recovering perfectionist, and my daughter and I have similar personalities.

I didn't want Gabriela to set her heart on this farm, because I didn't know how she could pull it off. If she couldn't buy it, I knew she would feel like she'd failed. And I've witnessed the way she turns on herself when she feels like a failure. She stomps around yelling "Dumb!" and "Stupid!" in reference to herself and makes dramatic and extreme statements like, "I'll *never* be able to do anything right!"

When this happens, what she needs is someone to take the time to listen, acknowledge that her feelings are normal, and hold her until she's done crying. I wish I could say I always do this. But sadly, I've often made things worse by raising my voice and going on and on about how she should stop being so hard on herself and *never* call herself names. And that if she wouldn't call her brother or her friend "stupid," then she shouldn't call herself "stupid" either, because to love your neighbor as yourself means you have to love yourself. Blah, blah, blah.

The hardest thing about raising kids is that they are like little mirrors, walking around showing us reflections of ourselves we'd rather not see. They probably reveal our good qualities as often as our bad, but most of the time the good stuff just goes over our heads until some saint of a person decides to point it out to us. Then for a fleeting moment we actually feel like good moms. You should spend as much time as is humanly possible with saints like these.

The bottom line with the farm was this: I didn't want Gabriela to fail. And I didn't want to fail Gabriela. Somewhere in the midst of wrestling my demons of perfectionism and my fear of becoming a colossal parenting failure, however, a ray of hope broke into my consciousness, or my husband's (we can't remember which) and we remembered the story of the little boy and his lunch.

At dinner Gabriela shared with the family her vision to buy a twenty-eight-animal farm that would help poor families get enough to eat and drink as well as have a way to earn extra income by selling the surplus eggs, milk, and offspring the animals would produce. We talked about how much money two thousand dollars was, and about the impossibility of her being able to go to school, do her homework, and still have enough time to do all the chores it would take to earn that much money. We also remembered a verse that one of the kids had learned at their private school: "Nothing is impossible with God" (Luke 1:37 NLT).

We talked about the story of Jesus and the little boy and his lunch, and we asked Gabriela what she thought her lunch was. What talent or gift did she think she could offer to God and ask Christ to do a miracle with? She thought about it for a minute, then said, "My art?"

Andy and I smiled. Fifteen minutes earlier we had thought of the same thing. "You know how we made Christmas cards for your grandparents last year using the drawing you did of Mary and baby Jesus," I said. "We could get a bunch of Christmas cards printed this year and sell them at church, in our neighborhood, and to our family and friends."

"This is a big amount of money, so you're going to have to involve a lot of people," Andy added. "Who else do you think could help you raise money for the farm?"

"Maybe my class at school."

"Maybe your Sunday school class," our four-year-old son chimed in.

"Maybe the school library, since Mrs. Richen is already giving us the idea to buy gifts from the World Vision catalog."

That night, and many nights to follow, we prayed around the dinner table and at bedtime that God would do a miracle and allow a second grader to raise two thousand dollars.

Gabriela talked to the librarian, who decided to make the farm the library's special Christmas project. Since Mrs. Richen gets to see every class in the school each week, she encouraged the entire student body to bring in money for the farm. We got a big glass jar and put pictures of farm animals on it, and we created a tracking chart so the kids could see how much money had come in and how much was still needed.

I asked a graphic designer friend if he could help with the Christmas card by framing Gabriela's artwork with a black border, putting a verse inside in a nice font, and adding a note on the back of the card, which explained that the proceeds from the card would go to World Vision.

Andy asked the choir director at the school where he works if Gabriela could sell her cards before and after the Christmas concert. The director said yes. I called an acquaintance who is involved with Women of Vision, the volunteer arm of World Vision. She was going to host the Women of Vision Christmas party in her home, so she asked me to bring over a bunch of cards to sell at the party.

A friend offered to sell Gabriela's cards at a Christmas bazaar. Another friend e-mailed all of her friends a scanned image of the card, took orders, and either shipped or delivered them herself. Our family sold the cards between services at our church during the four Sundays of Advent. I sold them at my women's Bible study. Lots of friends, family, and acquaintances bought Gabriela's cards. Two people from church wrote checks for one hundred dollars, and a stranger to us (a friend of a friend) wrote a check for three hundred.

I think we talked about the farm every night at dinner for two-and-a-half months. Sharing the victories and progress of the farm made for a unique and exciting season in our family's life, bringing us together around a common purpose and goal.

On Christmas morning we celebrated the miracle that we started praying for in October. Just over three thousand dollars had come in for the farm! My inner scrapbooker couldn't let this epic moment pass by undocumented, so I wrote a check for all the cash, put all the checks into a big envelope addressed to World Vision, and took a picture of Gabriela putting the envelope into the mailbox. This turned out to be anticlimactic because the envelope was too big for the slot in our cul-de-sac's mailbox. But at least we captured the spirit of the moment.

I buy each of our kids an ornament every Christmas to commemorate something special that happened during the year. Jonah got a Peter Pan ornament the year he dressed up as Peter Pan for Halloween and threw up on Andy while we were in line for the Peter Pan ride at Disney World. Gabriela got a Santa-riding-a-bicycle ornament the year she learned to ride her bike without training wheels; and a really cheesy-looking ornament of a librarian, with what looks like a fake tan, the year she learned to read.

Thanks to the exceptional timing of the brilliant people on Hallmark's ornament development team, the year we bought a farm Gabriela received a miniature ornament version of a Fisher Price farm on Christmas morning. The Fisher Price farm was one of my favorite childhood toys. My mom loved this toy so much she saved it for twenty-eight years so she could enjoy it all over again with her grandchildren. Gabriela's ornament even came with a tiny battery so that, like the toy, when you open the little barn doors, it moos.

I love the old proverb, "Put something where you can see it, so your eye will remind you heart." I hope this ornament will remind our family for decades to come of the year Gabriela bought the farm.

My children are raising me as much as I'm raising them. Parenthood is a messy, yet beautiful laboratory for spiritual formation—if I allow it to be.

Choose to Be

Jessica Kantola

Jessica Kantola has one four-year-old daughter, Siennalee McCall, and two houses. She looks forward to one day having more children and fewer houses.

She is a stay-at-home mom, a part-time graphic designer and photo editor for a local photographer, and an inconsistent blogger whose tidbits, tales, and tirades can be found at kantolafamilystory.blogspot.com.

I SAT slightly slumped, head in hand, staring out my kitchen window to the yard outside. I gazed at the blossoming pear tree my husband and I had planted the year after our first child, a daughter, was born, but I wasn't seeing it. Not really. My mind was busy working away at other thoughts. A breeze caught the petal-burdened branches and I blinked, a new thought forming: I would not see the tree reach its full potential. Things I planted and tended and loved would keep on growing, but I wouldn't be able to be a part of them. It was one more thing I was going to lose out on.

The thought was depressing.

It had been a full year of loss, beginning with having a shocking miscarriage, continuing on to adjusting to a major job change for my husband, putting our house on the market and preparing to move several hours away to an unfamiliar city, receiving news that my father-in-law was diagnosed with cancer, absorbing the heartbreak of a second miscarriage, navigating the continued stress of the house not selling and my husband absent during the work week, grieving for my sister-in-law as her marriage ended, then finally culminating with the death of my father-in-law.

The pain came like waves. I worked to stay afloat. And I waited for things to get better. Instead of new blessings and happy endings came the typical doldrums of life, including a leaking house and medical fears, all of which somehow gained new and scarier posturing when backed by the black hole of the past year.

*   *   *

"Be happy." It was one of my mother's favorite encouragements, doggedly given even during my darkest, teariest moments of adolescence. And if anybody ever had an excuse to be unhappy, it was my mom.

At eighteen, she left her family's Texas home and moved to California. She began to work for attorneys, her secretarial skills quickly growing into proficiency and then, wanting a change of scene, she moved up to Oregon where she met my dad. My dad, handsome, funny, and a bit of a bad boy, swept her off her feet and before she knew it she was married, and I was on my way. Unfortunately, the sweet little life she'd dreamed of was not to be. My dad, witty, charming, and talented, was also damaged and selfish. My mother alone could not hold her little family together. My parents divorced when I was twelve, fracturing a family that by then included two younger brothers.

My mother worked forty-plus hour weeks as a legal assistant for a well-known law office downtown. At times we had no car, so she—braving the weather—would walk several blocks to the city bus stop where she caught a bus for an hour commute to her office, then would repeat the trip, in reverse, at each day's end. My father offered no assistance, financial or otherwise. She put food on the table, clothes on our little growing bodies, and presents under the Christmas tree.

On weekdays she saw us only at nighttime, when she would come home, exhausted. Surely she longed for a nice dinner and a hot bath, but instead she would fix us a meal, clean us up, straighten the house, and squeeze out as much play time with her children as she could in the precious hours left before bedtime. She didn't date. Had no real hobbies. Wore second-and third-hand clothes. All her hard-earned resources were devoted to her children. She was the sole breadwinner, caretaker, and parent for myself and my two little brothers.

It could have been so depressing.

Yet my mother was always joyful. Quick to laugh. Ever pointing out the silver lining. On Saturday mornings she'd allow herself to be dragged from bed at ungodly hours for cartoons, collapse on the couch, and fall back to sleep surrounded by her three sleep-tousled children. She was the happiest then.

Now that I'm a married woman with a child of my own, I can look back and see with more clarity the details of her life. How hard it must have been to work in a posh law office with the latest fashions paraded by her while she wore shabby clothes from untold seasons back. There was no man to care for her, to ease her burdens, to listen to her confidences, or to simply wake up with her. When she found herself surrounded by couples in church and social settings, she was bound to feel the unfairness of her life. When she watched her children expectantly waiting by the door for a father who was prone to not show up for his preplanned visits, her heart must have broken.

Her life wasn't easy. But she never let it consume her — she never let it depress her. She continually searched out and found contentment and joy, despite her circumstances. "Be happy!" was her constant admonishment to my brothers and to me.

I remember my teenaged thoughts bemoaning how unfeeling it was for her to push me toward happiness when I was so dreadfully *un*happy—a breakup with a boyfriend, a low score on a test, yet another round of acne erupting across my face like Mount St. Helens. Surely she didn't understand. My life was *so* unfair. I was doomed to unhappiness. Yet still she pressed. "Be happy!" And I wasn't. "Be happy!" But my life was so awful. "Be happy!" And I began to see, slowly and aided by maturity, that it was not a feeling she pushed me toward, but a choice. She wasn't willing me to the *feeling* of being happy; she was teaching me that, despite circumstances, I could choose. I could choose to look for and grab hold of happiness, joy, and contentment in whatever place of life I might be. My mother's "be happy" meant "make the choice, and the feelings will follow."

*   *   *

"I don't want to go," I confessed heavily, my voice cracking as I finally broke into burning tears. I was facing down the nine-month deployment of my husband's U.S. Navy Reserve Unit to Kuwait. Nine months of being alone in a new house, in a new town, with a new baby. All alone. And with a post-natal body's unrelenting, on-going pain. My husband had already gone on ahead for his mobilization prep. I was readying to travel unaided with a six-month-old baby to the east coast for five weeks, staying with in-laws and in hotels. And preparing to say goodbye to my husband. Possibly forever. A military wife cannot afford naivety.

My mother listened. She herself was leaving for six months in Australia, and would not be available for me during my time of need. She was certainly more than sympathetic. She must have been so torn.

"Oh, but Jessica," she said, a quiet excitement brimming in her voice, "you can make it such an adventure!" She went on to retell the story of when she, alone, took a four-year-old me and my infant brother on the train from Oregon to Texas for a visit with her parents. As she once again related the familiar narrative, I began to see it in a different light. How stressful it could have been for her. How depressing. She was unsure if she would return to Oregon. She was attending to a new baby and a preschooler with no other adult support, and was in two seats on the rickety, rocking train for a good four days. Yet, save the instance I was trapped in between railcars, my memories of that trip are of nothing but excitement and adventure.

Seeing the story replay before me in a new light, I made up my mind right then. Now, if you look at pictures of my travels back east with my baby daughter, you'll see me smiling in each one. Not because I'm putting on a good face for the camera, or because I was willing myself into some sort of artificial happiness, but because I truly decided to make the heart-rending trip into a great adventure. My own memories and the stories I can tell of that trip are filled with excitement and adventure.

*   *   *

"Wake up, sweetie, good morning." I bend to nuzzle the warm, sleeping face of my three-year-old daughter. It is sometime before 6:00 a.m. and we are leaving for our week with Daddy, staying in the tiny, aged apartment we keep near his workplace, in the strange new city where we will be moving once our house sells. We need to leave early so he can still get to work at a decent time. It is just under a four-hour drive.

My daughter, unconcerned, sleeps peacefully on.

"Sweetheart, good morning." I rub her back and kiss her until she begins wriggling into her little wake-up sequence. Her small disheveled head comes up. Blue eyes blink groggily, "Is it morning time?"

"Yes, honey, it's time to get up so we can go," I murmur, thinking of my husband loading the last few things into our over-packed car and checking the clock to make sure we are still on schedule. I need to get her up and moving.

"Where we going?" Now she struggles into a sitting position and throws a chubby leg over the side of her almost too-small toddler bed.

"Down to spend our week with Daddy," I remind her, picturing the sparsely furnished apartment we'd dubbed "the geo-bachelor pad."

Her tiny face crumples, "Nooo!" Tears. She looks longingly back at her bed, then around at her familiar room, the air still tantalizingly heavy with sleep. "Nooo!" she cries again, sobbing in earnest now.

I know she is tired. So am I. I want to break down into messy tears too. Want to crawl back into my safe, familiar bed and stay there. I don't want to go out into the dark, cold world and drive down a road I don't know. I understand her tears. My heart breaks for my daughter.

But I shush her insistent "I don't wanna go" cries and brush her tears away.

Kissing her wet eyes and hugging her warm little body, I tell her, "This is a great adventure. Daddy is going to be so happy to have us with him for the week. We're going to have such fun...."

Soon we are dressed and giggling, still sleepy, still wanting home, but focusing on the happiness of going on an adventure with Daddy. With me in the lead, we are pushing past the heaviness of the moment and choosing to be joyful; we are creating a new moment ahead. We will choose not to focus on the things that aren't happening the way we want them to happen. We will choose to make the best of what we have right now.

My daughter will grow up with more than I had. New toys. New clothes. A doting daddy available and active in her life. My mother's lessons enriched my own life, but my daughter's life will be different. How will I model joy and contentment to her? How will I show her that happiness is born of choice, and is not merely a fleeting feeling to chase?

I do my best to practice it now—brushing away my own tears and searching out a silver lining to point out just above us. Acknowledging the sadness and losses of life, and then working hard to choose joy and expectant fulfillment for the empty places left behind. Hopefully, as my daughter watches me continue with my practicing, she will fall in step beside me and begin to understand that, like the most important things of life, contentment is a choice. It's the choice that remains after all the fiery things of life have burned themselves out.

Of course, I will still struggle with contentment. I may be the last person on earth who should be writing about it. My present season of life is not happening the way I'd hoped it would. Many days I feel despair circling. It can be almost impossible to muster feelings of happiness and joy. Then I look down into the glowing, expectant face of my daughter and remember I have a choice, despite feelings, despite circumstances. Even when brushing away my own tears can be like moving mountains. Even when acknowledging the sadness and losses of life and yet not letting them overwhelm can feel like fighting back the ocean tides. And always, little blue eyes watch me. So each day, I get to make a choice. I must weather this unwelcome season knowing that, inevitably, every season changes, but the choices we make during each season are what will stay with us.

I want my daughter to be able to look at the story of my life and understand that the continual choice for contentment is what allowed me to sow joy and happiness into our family, even through the dark years. I want my daughter to see that choosing contentment is what kept the garden of our lives freshly cultivated, no matter where we were planted and no matter what was growing—or waiting to grow—and that it was the choice for contentment that kept the soil of our family healthy, so that new life could flourish.

"Be happy!" I look forward to exhorting my daughter with the little secret code of my mother and me. I hope she can take my admonishment and remember watching me make the choices for happiness and contentment as she grew up. I want her to have the ability to survey life around her—the good and the bad, the side-splitting laughter and the heart-wrenching tears—and know that contentment is breathing all this in and choosing, despite whatever her feelings, circumstances, or the world around her says, to be at peace, fulfilled, and at rest.

Compromise

Valerie Weaver-Zercher

Valerie Weaver-Zercher recently edited the thirtieth-anniversary edition of *Living More with Less* (Herald Press, 2010), and her writing has been published in places like *Orion*, *Publishers Weekly*, *Christian Century*, and *Books & Culture*. Her work received special mention in the *Pushcart Prize XXXIII* anthology, and she was given a 2009 creative nonfiction fellowship from the Pennsylvania Council on the Arts.

Valerie lives in Mechanicsburg, Pennsylvania, with her husband and three sons.

> *"Let us not, then, take our littleness lightly.*
> *It is a wonderful grace." — Macrina Wiederkehr[1]*

A WEEK before Christmas, our oldest son—a kindergartener at the time—brought home a letter to Santa he had written at school. I found it that evening, stuffed at the bottom of his backpack, only after he and his little brothers had gone to bed. "Dear Santa," the worksheet read at the top, followed by a string of his large jutting letters, and then a parent volunteer's neat printing underneath. "I WNT THE SLN WO," wrote Sam.

Clueless, and thankful for a translation, I read on. "I want the soldiers of," wrote the volunteer, and then the adult writing stopped. They must have been in a hurry and decided he could finish at home, I thought, wondering what he had intended to communicate. "I want the soldiers of….I want the soldiers of…." I mumbled, carrying the paper to the kitchen to show my husband.

Then its meaning hit me, and I opened my mouth in surprise and pride. He must have been starting to write, "I want the soldiers *out* of *Iraq*!" He and his brother Isaiah had been asking lots of questions about the Iraq War recently: when it would end, where Baghdad was, who lived in Iraq, what the people looked like, and why the war was going on. While being careful to shelter them from visual images of the war and making sure they felt safe and secure, my husband and I tried to mete out age-appropriate doses of information, both to satisfy their curiosity and to begin sharing with them our pacifist perspectives.

And now, here was proof that we were doing the pacifist parenting thing just right! Here was our kindergartener, writing to Santa that all he wanted for Christmas was for the soldiers to come home from Iraq! I felt overcome with pride at my little activist, already joining the movement at the tender age of five. I knew our recent emphasis on Advent wreaths and relief kits for refugee children, rather than on the newest Shrek movie and trips to see Santa, would pay off.

"Look at this!" I said, waving Sam's Santa letter, walking into the kitchen where my husband was baking pumpkin pies. "You won't believe what Sam did in school today."

It was only as I began to read the letter out loud that another possibility struck me like a full-size front-loader scoop of Duplos. Suddenly I knew the truth—and it sure as heck didn't set me free. Sam had not planned to write "I want the soldiers out of Iraq," but rather, "I want the soldiers of Spencer."

The week before, he had played with toy soldiers at his friend Spencer's house, setting them up in complex battle configurations, hauling them in the back of a pickup truck to "the war at New Cumberland Valley," and designating some of the little blue plastic guys as videographers to record the battle for the training of new recruits (which we recently discovered had been Theodor Geisel's job in World War II, before he became Dr. Seuss). Then Sam had spent the entire trip home whining about how we didn't have any fun toys like soldiers or guns.

I banged my forehead at my own naiveté while my husband guffawed over his pumpkin custard. He knows the way I set myself up for such falls, the way my stratospheric ideals for parenting have nowhere to go but down. Sure enough, the next day when I asked Sam what he intended to write, he confirmed he had indeed set out to ask Santa for toy soldiers. (Less than a week later he would politely feign excitement at the Scrabble game Santa picked up at Target instead.)

I shouldn't have been surprised. In the last month alone Sam had turned the clove apple we were making for Christmas into a gun ship, made Mary and the shepherds in our crèche set have a manger-side rumble, and turned cardboard boxes into armor for a medieval body-slamming contest. Granted, he was a well-rounded five-year-old who also liked woodworking, soccer, coloring, and checkers. Still, I could no longer deny the truth: From all indications, my eldest son was headed not to the Peace Corps but straight for Camp Lejeune.

I am not alone in my befuddlement at a son's interest in guns, thankfully; entire books have been written to help parents deal constructively with our children's banana-turned-gun games.[2] Many experts suggest engaging a child's war fantasies and encouraging the creative outworking of such play (as long as it doesn't involve younger siblings, rope, and duct tape). Banning imaginary violent play altogether can lend it the exciting aura of the forbidden, as well as short-circuit the opportunity to help children sort out fantasy and reality, develop political and moral ideas, and learn to cooperate and consider other points of view.[3] But as fascinated as I am by such discussions of children's violent play, I am much more interested in my own disillusionment that my son engages in it.

Before becoming a mother, I would have sworn that my children would not even know what a gun was when they were five years old, let alone draft complicated battle plans for toy soldiers. I was convinced I could raise sons in a creative and peaceable environment such that violent play simply wouldn't occur to them; they'd be too busy making bran muffins for the shut-ins at church and building homeless shelters out of couch pillows.

Nine years into parenting, I'm drawing the lines at much more modest places. I still don't buy my kids toy guns, but I also don't dictate what my son plays with at a friend's house. Nor have I decreed an end to the production of homemade weapons ingeniously crafted out of play dough, Legos, and rubber bands. And here's the confession extraordinaire: I let my sons use their saved-up allowance money to buy Nerf guns. I actually did.

My retreat from the territory of ideal pacifist parenting is due to many factors: exhaustion, the awareness that constant refusals from me will create only heightened desire in my sons, and the knowledge that rigid limits on the scope of their play teaches them that creativity should be constrained. Before I had kids, of course, all of this would have sounded like a bunch of hooey.

In a study of a group of liberal, well-educated middle-class mothers in London, anthropologist Daniel Miller found that his subjects experienced parenting as "a series of inevitable defeats."[4] He outlines the battles that occurred between mothers and infants on two fronts—food and gender—and the disillusionment that the mothers articulated at their loss of control over their children's behavior. In the food battle, babies reared on breastmilk and strained organic sweet potatoes suddenly fixated on the Coca-Cola and Smarties from which the parents could not, in the end, entirely protect them. On the gender front, infants whom the mothers carefully dressed in green and yellow suddenly wanted to play with only dolls or only trucks (you guess who wanted which).[5]

Miller suggests that, within the community of alternative mothers he studied, parenting "becomes a form of tragic practice, in which—as when infants vainly attempt to stem the tide with sandcastles—parents obsessively attempt to build dams and repair breaches through which pour the growing agency and autonomy of their infants."[6]

Raising precious children as "tragic practice": What could be more depressing? Yet if my experiences, those of my friends, and those of the mothers in Miller's study are any indication, the smack-down of ideals is not only an occasional occurrence in parenting but a guaranteed and regular feature of it. And within the framework of idealism out of which many new parents operate—especially those who are committed to justice, peace, and simplicity—what could be more tragic than compromise?

One way to get beyond the faulty algebra of idealized parenting is to refer to an alternate meaning of *compromise*. I usually think of the negative connotation of the word, the one that means "capitulation," or the surrender of principles. There is another, more positive meaning, of course, and one that may be instructive here: Compromise involves *negotiation* of a conflict, and the process of giving up one goal in order to obtain another one. It calls to mind the balancing of mutually exclusive objectives, or the calculated trading of one value for another.

When I worked at a mediation center in the 1990s, compromise was seen as a second-rate solution. The climate in the mediation field was one of optimism that all parties in most conflicts could win without losing any of their deeply held values. The subtitle to the most popular book in the field said it all: "Negotiating Agreement Without Giving In."[7] Compromise was the unfortunate and uninformed cousin of *collaboration* and *transformation*; if the parties in any conflict just worked a little harder, empathized a little more, talked a little longer, they could reach an agreement whereby all would emerge happy, or at least satisfied that their needs had been met. Compromisers were also seen as slightly manipulative because of their willingness to "give a little to get a little"; one conflict type test I used in mediation trainings associated a fox, because of its slyness, with this style of resolving conflict.

Somehow along the way (I'll wager it happened around February 21, 2001, when my first son was born), I lost my end-of-the-first-millennium optimism, both in actual win-win solutions and also in the metaphoric role they play in these reflections on parental compromise. I do not doubt that win-win solutions can be found for some conflicts, or that two ostensibly conflicting ideals can at times be juggled without dropping one of them. Yet I'm increasingly frustrated by the notion that it is *always* possible to hold together *all* of one's ideals in perfect harmony, without one ideal hauling off and slapping another one upside the head. Ideals—at least those in my head—can be as scrappy as people. They're tough guys, impervious to criticism, and don't take kindly to soft words like *mediating* and *negotiating*.

But one of the wisest things a spiritual director told me, during a year when I was beginning to make out the catch-22s of socially conscious parenting on my horizon, was that sometimes we need to clutch some of our values more tightly and others more loosely. A choice to embrace one ideal may mean that another has to be held at arm's length, at least temporarily. For example: Living in a racially diverse city that is also twenty miles from your workplace means using up gas and spending forty minutes in a car instead of with your family. Living close to where you work, on the other hand, may mean living in a homogenous, middle-class suburb. Hanging the clothes out to dry and washing dishes by hand may mean you can't put a puzzle together with your preschooler that afternoon, let alone write; using your dryer and your dishwasher, on the other hand, means using up fossil fuels. Volunteering overnight at a homeless shelter (and getting two hours of sleep) may mean that the next day that you sit the kids down in front of a screen so you can sleep; not volunteering anywhere means you further insulate yourself from the realities of the world. Assuming that the values of each commitment never conflict with the values of others is as naïve as thinking that people who love each other will never argue.

My sister had pledged that she would never give any baby of hers a pacifier. Like many expectant parents committed to natural childbirth and childrearing, she saw pacifiers as pathetic rubber substitutes for a mother's breast that inhibited mother-child bonding, messed with breastfeeding, and introduced toxins into a child's body. She watched graciously as my husband and I tossed aside our own convictions against pacifiers in the face (literally) of three sons who all had what we diagnosed as "excessive sucking needs." But I could tell she thought we were lightweights.

In the first few weeks after her first son's birth, she and her husband valiantly strove to avoid the pacifiers that two grandmothers colluded to leave lying around their house. Their fussy newborn sucked on their upturned pinkies, nursed nonstop, was bounced around in the sling, sucked on a grandpa's pinky, breastfed some more, sucked on some aunts' and uncles' pinkies, and treated his mother's nipples like they were as vital as air—all while his parents' resolve slowly melted into a puddle of fatigue and frustration at their feet. I couldn't help but smile when I saw my hearty seven-month-old nephew on one visit, happily chewing away on his binky like it was a cut of prime rib. It was even clipped to his shirt in case he dropped it from his mouth (about as likely as an alcoholic spitting out beer).

It is hard not to smirk a tiny bit in watching my sister and my friends, one by one, laid low by the parental compromises born of profound exhaustion and the surprising agency of very short people who cannot yet eat an entire meal without falling off their chairs. There is a more than a hint of schadenfreude here; apparently compromise loves company as much as misery does.

But my amusement at new parents' emerging humility is mixed with empathy, because I remember traversing the same terrain of sadness, fatigue, and disillusionment as I watched my smugly built edifice of ideals crumble to the ground. Six years into parenting, I could quickly laugh at my own hubris as revealed in my first reading of Sam's Santa letter. In early parenthood, however, as I watched the slow but certain burn of my parenting ideals, there was no humor and only pain.

But I am learning this: When watching friends eat the humble pie of parenting, do not ask how it tastes. Do not comment on the pacifier, or Barbie, or toy soldiers, or hour of screen time. Consider the pain of parenting as tragic practice, and hold your tongue.

ENDNOTES

1. Macrina Wiederkehr, *A Tree Full of Angels* (San Francisco, CA: HarperCollins, 1988), 27.

2. See Nancy Carlsson-Paige and Diane E. Levin, *Who's Calling the Shots? How to Respond Effectively to Children's Fascination with War Play and War Toys* (Philadelphia, PA: New Society Publishers, 1990).

3. Ibid., 35-37.

4. Daniel Miller, "How Infants Grow Mothers in North London," in *Consuming Motherhood,* ed. Janelle S. Taylor, et. al (New Brunswick, NJ: Rutgers, 2004), 48.

5. Miller suggests reasons other than simply the old "girls-and-boys-are-different" argument to explain this gendered preference of toys. He surmises that the claiming of gender by children within a feminist household "may be just as effective a symbol of autonomy as the refusal of gender has been for children brought up in families with a strong gender ideology" (42).

6. Ibid., 48.

7. See Roger Fisher, et. al, *Getting to Yes: Negotiating Agreement Without Giving In* (New York, NY: Penguin, 1991).

In the World

"A new command I give you:
Love one another. As I have loved you,
so you must love one another."

(John 13:34 NIV)

The Day We
Let Our Son Live

Ellen Hsu

Ellen Hsu is the mother of two boys, Josiah (8) and Elijah (5).

She is the subsidiary rights manager for InterVarsity Press, where she enjoys working with people from around the world involved in publishing and literature ministry. She is also a volunteer worship leader at Church of the Savior (West Chicago, Illinois).

I GAZED in wonder at the blurry form on the screen. "Hi, Baby," I whispered. The image of our baby was much clearer on the level-two ultrasound. The technician rolled the ultrasound wand over my growing abdomen, now slippery with gel, and I marveled as I watched our son squirm a bit and suck his thumb.

A new life forming within me.

Al was supposed to be with me at the doctor's office, but was running late after discovering his car had a flat tire. I hoped he would arrive in time to see the clearer images of our son. Our OB/GYN referred us for a level-two ultrasound after noticing choroid plexus cysts on our baby's brain during the standard twenty-week ultrasound. I was anxious about what the maternal-health specialist might find. We knew a couple whose ultrasound also showed choroid plexus cysts, but whose baby was perfectly fine when he was born. We had spent the past week praying for our baby and hoping for the best.

Al walked into the exam room as the technician was finishing up. She hadn't said much while she worked, and explained that the doctor would be in to take a look for himself and to explain what he found. Al and I chatted quietly while we waited. I was relieved Al had made it before the doctor came in. Little did I know how much I would need him.

The doctor came in and began his exam. I was delighted at the chance to see more images of our baby. But my world was shaken when the doctor finally began explaining what he saw. "Something is very wrong with this baby."

He continued to roll the wand over my tummy as he pointed to various spots on the screen and began listing all of the "abnormalities" he found. Larger than usual nuchal folds… clenched fists…possible club feet…something wrong with the liver…enlarged ventricles in the brain…no stomach (but maybe he just couldn't see it yet because the baby was so small). My tears flowed as his list grew longer. My delight at the new life within me turned to icy fear and I clutched Al's hand tightly.

The doctor suspected a chromosomal problem, possibly Trisomy 13 or 18, birth defects caused by an extra thirteenth or eighteenth chromosome. The doctor explained that both of these conditions are generally "incompatible with life." We were told that if our baby was born alive, he was likely to die within a day. If we were lucky, he might survive for six to twelve months. We wondered if we should begin preparing for death instead of life.

Frightened and uncertain of our baby's future, we agreed to an amniocentesis. We would not, we thought, consider aborting our child, but we wanted to know what to expect. And this situation wasn't really covered in *What to Expect When You're Expecting*. Al held my hand while the doctor extracted amniotic fluid from my womb using a long needle. The procedure was over quickly and the baby seemed to be okay, that is, if you didn't count all of his "abnormalities." The doctor explained that it would take around two weeks to receive the results and mentioned when we would need to make a decision regarding termination.

Once we were home I went to our bedroom and wept. I left Al to explain to his mom what was wrong; she was watching our three-year-old for us that day. I was worried she would blame me.

Later that evening, after we'd both had some time to process the news, Al and I talked. I felt lost. This scenario didn't fit any of my plans and I had no idea how to respond. We talked about funerals and, if the baby survived, what life would be like for us and for him.

"What should we do?" I asked. "I never thought I would even think this, but do you think it would be more compassionate to terminate the pregnancy?" I felt horrible even thinking about abortion, but given what the doctor told us I honestly wondered which was the more loving thing to do: save him from the pain and difficulties he would likely experience if he survived, or allow him to live.

After a moment of silence Al responded, "I think we should do no harm." Relieved, I quietly agreed. From that moment on we began to prepare ourselves to welcome our son into this world, no matter what that looked like. The most important day in my life is the day we decided to let our son live.

We chose a name and began to refer to our son as Elijah instead of "the baby." It helped us to remember that he was "real." Even if he didn't survive the pregnancy, he was alive now and we would enjoy him as long as we could.

A couple of weeks later, shortly before Christmas, the doctor called with the results of the amniocentesis. Elijah was diagnosed with Trisomy 21, more commonly known as Down syndrome, a condition caused by an extra twenty-first chromosome. We had done some research. We knew that a diagnosis of Down syndrome meant that Elijah would have difficulty learning. We knew that he would experience developmental delays, such as walking and talking later than typical children. We also knew he was more likely to have a congenital heart defect and other medical problems.

The doctor asked if we had made a decision regarding termination. I was surprised. "What? Why would we terminate? It's only Down syndrome!" I was actually relieved. Elijah would most likely survive. I had no idea at the time that close to 90 percent of people who receive a pre-natal diagnosis of Down syndrome decide to terminate their pregnancy.

Although we were glad Elijah would most likely live, we still grieved our lost hopes for a "perfect" baby. I vacillated between mourning, "This is not what I planned for my life!" and making new plans. I spent many evenings crying (pregnancy hormones were bad enough, but a difficult diagnosis made things even worse!). We read whatever books we could find about Down syndrome. We contacted the National Association for Down Syndrome (NADS) and were paired with a support family. I was put on partial bed rest and spent much time at the maternal health specialist's office for appointments and non-stress tests.

On April 8, thirty-seven weeks into the pregnancy, I went to see the maternal health specialist for a standard appointment. I told him I was a little worried because Elijah wasn't moving very often. Since Elijah was technically full-term, the doctor decided we should deliver him via C-section. I was promptly taken to a hospital room where I called Al and told him that we were having a baby. Today!

A few hours later Al held newborn Elijah Timothy Hsu up for me to see. He was small, just four pounds seven ounces, and looked like a little old man. I had a few moments to gaze at him before the nurses took him to the NICU (Neonatal Intensive Care Unit). After several difficult weeks, Elijah was released from the hospital, and we took him home.

Other than Down syndrome, most of the other "abnormalities" the doctor listed were not present. Today Elijah is a happy and healthy five-year-old. He loves school, can read picture books, and is learning some math. He communicates using a combination of sign language and spoken words. He enjoys giving hugs, dancing, and playing computer games. His smile lights up a room and his laugh is contagious. He and his eight-year-old brother, Josiah, play and fight together like any siblings. He also gets into trouble, like any five-year-old might. He's broken some of our things, sometimes spills his milk, and once he colored on our white furniture with a purple marker.

What has surprised me most about Elijah is how he is more "normal" than he is different. He has developmental delays and it sometimes takes him longer to learn new skills, but for the most part he's just a normal kid doing normal kid stuff. Elijah's first year was sometimes difficult and overwhelming, but life with Elijah has settled into its own routine. Taking care of him is not all that different from taking care of our typical child. And loving Elijah comes just as naturally to me as loving Josiah.

I can't imagine life without Elijah anymore. He brings us so much joy. I'm so glad he's alive and that he's a part of our family. And I look forward to the day when Elijah can tell me about the most important day of his life.

The Heat Is On

Shari MacDonald Strong

Shari MacDonald Strong lives in Portland, Oregon, and is the mother of five children.

Her work has appeared in *Geez*, Mamazine.com, *Jesus Girls*, and AustinMama.com, among other places. She is the former spiritual columnist at LiteraryMama.com. Her book, *The Maternal is Political*, was published by Seal Press in 2008.

IT'S THE HOTTEST week of the summer, with each of the last two days topping 100 degrees. Even at night, the heat is nearly unbearable, so my husband and I seek the solace of an air-conditioned theater with our three children and some friends. As we exit the theater at 9:30 p.m., the air is heavy and thick: near 90 degrees, still.

We part ways with some of our friends and trudge back to our van with another. On the way, my husband glances at a red sports car parked at the curb, pausing to peer closely at something tucked under one of the windshield wipers: a flyer advertising a downtown club, I speculate. Then he grabs the paper and holds it up for our friend Susan and me to inspect: "God Doesn't Want You to Go to Hell," the leaflet says. "Doesn't Want You" is in tiny letters between "God" and "Hell." Red flames lick at the bottom of the words. My husband crumples the paper in his hands.

"Good for you," says Susan. "You're my hero." All three of us have seen the tracts, have heard the message, thousands of times before—"Turn or Burn"—and his gesture is one part act of compassion, one part public service. Each of us spent years being sad or confused or frightened about, or feeling rejected by, a wrathful God. As a teenager, I had nightmares for years after being subjected at youth group to *A Thief in the Night*: the film version of an evangelistic tract, about how God returns during the rapture to separate husbands and wives, mothers and children, taking up to heaven all those who said the right words in the right order, in the right prayer, leaving everyone else on earth to suffer through a deadly tribulation.

I know what it's like to live for years with the anguish of fearing eternal damnation. I prayed to ask Jesus into my heart at least a dozen times between ages eight and twenty-eight; if you believe in a God so wrathful, so angry, it's hard to believe saying the right phrase or formula will actually save your soul. My husband and I, like our friend Susan, feel healthier now, more secure in who we are and what we believe, decades after being introduced to a fear-based spirituality as children. But it took us a long time to get here.

"What are you doing?" my eight-year-old daughter asks, watching my husband. Her little brothers are laughing and playing on the sidewalk; I can't tell if they noticed Craig's actions.

"That's a mean note," I explain to any of them who are listening. "The person who drives this car doesn't need to read a mean note."

We all walk past the next car, and my husband snatches a hellfire-and-brimstone tract off of that one too. We make our way past vans, compact cars, pick-up trucks. Pretty soon, Craig has a fistful of paper. Even my daughter has managed to grab one of the offending pamphlets.

"Let's throw them away," one of us says, and we make our way toward a garbage can.

"I want to throw one away!" and "Me, too!" my children shout. We grown-ups glance at one another and shrug and hand them the papers, making sure that the tracts go directly into the trash can—that the children don't have a chance to stop and get a better look.

A couple of blocks farther, at the corner of the downtown square, we come across two people handing out tiny flyers. My children are happily running a dozen feet ahead of us on the sidewalk, and they glance at the pair—a young man, maybe twenty-three, and a girl of about twenty, pretty, with long, dark hair. The two step toward my children, and I see what the papers are. The girl puts a picture of hellfire into the hand of my five-year-old son while the man looks on approvingly.

"No," I say, startled.

"Give it back," my husband says sternly, and our son looks at us, unworried but curious.

"No!" I say again, and our five-year-old gently puts the tract back into the girl's hand. I shoo my children ahead of me, like a frightened, enraged hen—protecting their innocence, their mental health, their intuitive faith in unconditional love.

"What are those?" the children ask.

"They're papers that say hateful things," says Susan. "We want people to read loving things, not hateful things."

As we load the children in the van a few blocks later, I'm shaking.

"How disgusting that they'd give that *to a five-year-old,*" my husband says to me.

"I'm tempted to go back there and say something," I threaten.

"Okay," my husband tells me, and I kind of think he's kidding. But he drives right up to the square and pulls over.

I climb out of the van and, despite my natural tendencies toward conflict-avoidance, march up to the two offenders, fueled by adrenaline and outrage. Across the street, on my right, several more zealots stand at the corner. Two men, side by side, shout nearly identical threats about repentance and hellfire and damnation; one has a small P.A. system, and he perches at the edge of the curb, staring aggressively into cars stopped at the light as he shouts into a microphone. I wait for a moment, pick my battle, and turn back to the couple who'd held out the tracts to my family.

"Don't you *ever* give those to children again," I say, and there is fire in my voice.

The man looks amused. "Why not?" He is barely stifling a smirk. He is young and full of false superiority. The young woman beside him stands silently.

"Because they're children. You don't hand children something that tells them God hates them, and they're going to hell."

"It doesn't say that. It says *God doesn't want them to go to hell.*" He waves his tract at me triumphantly: Exhibit A. He's very proud. I have to squint to read the word "Doesn't."

He shrugs as I'm about to turn away. "Fine. I won't give them to *your* children."

I spin back around. "To *any* children. Children don't need to be subjected to your nastiness and your hatred."

"Why? All we want is to see people in heaven."

"Well, if that's what you want, you're going about it the wrong way."

"I've seen people get saved because they got these tracts!"

"Are you kidding me?" I ask. "Do you have any idea how this stuff spoils Christianity? How it drives people away from the church? I'm a Quaker. I like Jesus. *I love Jesus!* But it's *humiliating* to be associated with people like you. You just utterly ruin it for everybody!" I am waving wildly, punctuating my sentences with the sweep of an arm, pointing toward my kids, who watch from the van, some thirty feet away.

"I've spent years trying to teach my children that God is loving, and you are just going to sweep in and destroy that with your talk about hell and your pictures of fire?"

"You know, I think you're the one who's nasty," the man says. He is starting to lose his cool. He isn't meeting my eyes anymore. He folds his arms across his chest and leans back, giving me a look of disgust. His tone is hard, and his female companion's affect is so blank, for a moment I consider quitting religion on the spot, forever.

I fold my own arms and mimic his look, momentarily mirroring his posture and glare. "Well," I say, straightening again, "that's not nearly as nasty as telling people that God hates them and is sending them to hell."

"That's what the Bible says!"

"You know, your God is going to have a talk with you," I say. "Because you're very confused. Why do you have to take the meanest, nastiest possible interpretation of everything?" I look at the woman, who is still staring back at me wordlessly, and I feel a mixture of anger and sympathy. "You should be ashamed of yourselves. *Keep this stuff away from children.*" As I storm away, I'm shaking, and I feel sick to my stomach.

"Why were they handing out those papers?" my children ask when I get back in the van, and I take a breath to calm myself.

My daughter says, "God doesn't hate anyone." She thinks for a moment. "You know what you could have done?" she says. "You could have asked for a bunch of those papers, and then thrown them away!"

"You're right," I say, smiling a little. "That's a good idea. I should have done that." My husband reaches out and holds my hand as he drives us home. I consider calling the non-emergency police line and reporting that religious group for harassment, and my children think this is a grand idea. But my husband points out that zealots just love being made into martyrs, and I know he's right. I decide not to make the call.

"Did those people listen to you?" my children ask.

"They weren't really listeners," I say.

I wish my children could have watched us somehow right the wrong we stumbled across, and in the absence of a solution I feel helpless and sad. "You know, sometimes," I say to my children, "you can't really stop something bad that's going on. Sometimes you just have to say something for the sake of saying it, because saying something is all you can do." I'm glad my children saw three grown-ups they love speak up against what was happening; they saw me do the only thing I could: use my voice.

In the next minute, the conversation shifts, and my children begin to talk about other things, not the slightest bit upset about the exchange, though it will stick with me for the rest of the night. We drive back home in the sweltering heat, and my husband puts the children right to bed, because in the morning, they have church, where I hope and believe they'll learn about God, who manifests love and inclusiveness and generosity. Then my husband opens all the windows to the waning heat, and he turns on the fan in the windowsill to get a breeze going. And I lie down on the bed and take deep breaths, reassured by the promise of a wind so warm and so faint you wouldn't even know it was there unless you were looking for it.

Being the Light

Becky Towne

Becky Towne is the mother of four children—Halee (30), Jimmy (29), Dylan (28), and Carly (28)—and has enjoyed being a mother-in-law for two years to Mara, Dylan's wife.

Becky recently completed sixteen years as senior editor of *The Friends Voice*, a national newsletter for Evangelical Friends Church—North America, and is associate dean and associate professor of Christian spirituality at Houston (Texas) Graduate School of Theology.

I FOUND myself in a dilemma. Some of my friends were homeschooling their children, and although I liked the basic concept of homeschooling (and still do), I was unsettled about that route for our family. We moved from Texas to Iowa when our children were young, and the small community where my husband pastored had its own elementary school, just a block away from our new parsonage.

Jim and I discussed the potential ramifications of our choices regarding schooling. We were reminded that, as followers of Christ, we were to be lights in the world, shining like stars. Therefore, we concluded, our responsibility was to train up our children and send them out into their worlds as light— not later when they were "all grown up," but now when we could be in conversation with them as their parents. To be light in their schools, our children would learn to be compassionate and to value the unpopular kids. They would reflect our practices of simplicity and stewardship. Most of all, they would discover the importance of struggling with and relating to peers from a variety of backgrounds and situations. Part of our responsibility would be involvement in the school system as much as we could.

The decision was made. Our children would attend public school.

I volunteered in the PTA of the new school and became treasurer. I got to know the principal, teachers, and staff, and was soon asked to play piano for the elementary school choir. Jim coached baseball teams and attended every choir program and sports event possible.

I noticed changes in our family that first year of school. Our three younger children waited at the door for our oldest daughter, Halee, to return home. They wanted to hear about her experiences on her own. Carly, our second, especially hung on every word when her big sister returned home to teach Carly everything she could remember from her day.

Our twin boys were equally excited about school. Jimmy could barely wait for his turn to leave the herd and get out on his own, but kindergarten was disappointing to him at first. He had envisioned having lots of friends and getting to do so many new things.

Just after mid-year, we kept Jimmy home from school with a respiratory infection on a very cold day. On the way back from an appointment with our doctor, tears came to his eyes as he admitted, "Mom, I don't have any friends. The other kids must not like me."

Our hearts were broken for him, but I did my best to reassure him, "Oh, Jimmy, you are such a great kid. You will find a friend soon." Then I prayed that God would bring a friend into Jimmy's life.

His friend turned out to be a little blonde boy who loved to play tether ball. Earlier that year, we found a tether ball pole, which had been cemented into a tire, and brought it home so the kids would have something to do outside. Soon, our house was the site for tether-ball tournaments with the little blonde boy. Word about the backyard tether-ball games got out, and soon many new friends entered our lives.

As the years went by, I was aware that each of the four children loved discovering who they were and what they could do apart from the family. The addition of friends, invitations to parties, and breaking out of what had been our family life was a fun and welcomed change—until middle school. By that time, we had moved to Colorado Springs where Jim pastored another Friends church.

In our new location, our sweet, gentle children encountered other children who had vastly different backgrounds than they had. They rode the bus, heard derogatory names, and found themselves unsure about how to be themselves in this new situation. Some days I found myself longing for the more rural setting of eastern Iowa.

We continued to talk with them about bringing the light of Christ into the schools, while in our own hearts we wondered about our decision to keep our children in public school. Aware of the potential pitfalls, trials, and consequences of our decision, we knew that we couldn't protect our children from the challenges of life. We did have those twelve crucial schooling years, however, in which we could walk with them through the difficulties, before they set out on their own.

Four high school teenagers in one household provided even more challenges. Our lives were full of concerts, plays, games, orthodontist appointments, cars, and discussions—lots of them—about the kids' struggles in carrying the light of

Christ into their situations. The results weren't always positive. Friends continued to be important to all four children. Most of Jimmy's friends were from single-parent families and seemed to have more freedom than our children were allowed. He moved out the day he turned eighteen to live with some of his friends and experience more of their lives. Dylan's friends were not always appreciated by other teens. His buddies were short, pudgy, and unpopular. Our tall, thin Dylan struggled with his own desires to be accepted. I pondered and prayed about our decisions regarding our four amazing children, continuing to wonder if we had done the right thing in our earlier choice to keep them in public schools.

Then God spoke the answer to my wondering, twenty-eight years after the birth of our twin boys. The answer came independently from my two daughters, during discussions about school-day memories. They both referred to being sent out to be light into their schools. I didn't think they would even remember those words.

Today, Carly's desire is to minister to people who would probably not visit a church. She has a great many friends, and sometimes the line gets blurred between bringing the light of Christ into dark situations and allowing the darkness to affect her life. I wonder whether our years of conversations about the difficulties of bringing light in school have helped us be honest in our questions and answers together regarding her current friends and lifestyle choices.

Dylan is married. He and his wife are both spiritually minded people with thoughtful questions and interests. They are interested in Quaker theology and discovering how that applies to their lives. Because Dylan is a chef, working late into the night and on weekends, he struggles with attending Sunday-morning church services. Because of his career in the food-service industry, however, he is still drawn to the marginalized, being more missional and available than many who make it to church each Sunday morning.

Jimmy has maintained relationships with his good friends from high school. One day, not long after he moved out, he complained about his friends' lack of decorum regarding keeping the kitchen and bathroom of their apartment clean. We talked about the difference it makes when a person is brought up to respect others by cleaning up his or her own mess. He realized that he was brought up differently from his friends, and he thought a little differently about our household after that. He joins the family in worship while he continues to process his own relationship with God.

Halee, an elementary school music teacher, is also trained in vocal performance and musical theater. She considers the messages of the musicals for which she auditions. She doesn't always make the choices I would make regarding those musicals, but nevertheless, she radiates the light of Christ to her theater friends and finds a variety of ways to minister in that setting.

I don't know if my children are more missional in their approaches than their homeschooled peers, but I do know that as they continue to struggle with life, they work to think through their choices. The relationships we now enjoy are enriched because of the important conviction, discussions, and challenges relating to being the light in school that we faced together.

Some days, I wish I had a more storybook ending to share about our decision to send out our children to be light in their schools, but maybe my ideas of what constitutes good endings are not what God sees as good endings. I remember that I was called to be a faithful follower of Jesus, not a writer of happily-ever-afters. The results of my attempts at obedience and the continuation of my children's stories are in God's hands. I pray that we will all be light in our worlds—schools, churches, theater, and workplaces. And I long for and anticipate that day when I will learn that my children have talked to their children about being light in their schools too.

Gun Control

Doreen Dodgen-Magee

Doreen Dodgen-Magee is the mother of Connor and Kaija and wife of Thomas. She relishes celebrating people and collecting unique experiences. A psychologist in private practice, she maintains a busy public-speaking docket and is passionate about empowering people to live countercultural, relationally rich lives.

Her insights on the impact of technology on families can be found at doreendm.com.

TWELVE, and full of seventh-grade machismo, Connor hopped in the van after school with a mind full of ideas and a mouth full of plans. Sharing excitedly about his day, his diatribe ended with, "And all the guys and I have been talking, and I know what I want to do with my allowance. There's a new airsoft gun I want to buy." In a flash I became angry and agitated. Airsoft guns, which are realistic-looking guns that shoot small, round pellets and are used by middle school and high school boys to play "war," were all the rage at the time. Any gathering of boys was sure to be peppered with talk of models of such guns and descriptions of face masks and other padding made to protect one from the inevitable bruises that come with a good backyard battle.

We had discussed "airsofting" at length in our home by this time. Connor had made a case for buying a gun and we, very reluctantly, let him use his own money to purchase one—with several clear stipulations. One: The gun could not look real. (He chose a clear plastic model with bright-colored insides, like a crazy water gun. It met our criteria.) Two: He could only use the toy when we approved of the people with whom he was playing. Three: We were not willing to tolerate this activity becoming an object of his obsession. The gun and one package of pellets would be his limit. We were not willing to entertain further pleading or incessant talk about the newest and most advanced guns, accessories, or strategies for "fighting." And the stipulation supreme: We wanted to hear from him, as he engaged with this activity, how he aligned his desire to play war with his self-proclaimed pacifistic ideals. For me, this was the most important issue, and I wanted it addressed sooner rather than later.

Weeks passed and Connor fought a few battles. Bruises marking where he'd been hit healed, and still, nothing about his views on pacifism and airsoft guns changed. He just didn't see the connection, he said. He was just playing a game, no different from the board game "Risk," only with "running and moving," he said. He also said he was drawn to the features on a new model of gun.

That's where everything went south.

In the van, while Connor was merely commenting on what he'd been immersed in all day, conversing with friends, I found myself thrown wildly and deeply into a hole of unresolved pain. Ten years earlier my world had been rocked by a gun. This gun issued real, life-taking bullets, was far from bright and colorful, and was wielded by an angry and vindictive individual. The weapon's similarities to *all* guns deeply impacted my ability to be neutral regarding all L-shaped objects with triggers and barrels. On this particular occasion in the van with my son, I completely lost my ability to respond rationally.

"When *you* have dealt with the death of your sister and nieces to gun-shot wounds made by their husband and father, *then* you can buy a new gun! When *you* have cleaned your three-month-old nieces' blood out of your mother-in-law's hair, *then* you can buy a new gun! When *you* are mature enough to understand how ridiculous you and your friends are, and you understand the idiocy of this 'game,' *then you can buy a stupid new gun!*"

The words came flooding out of me. Involuntary, loud, angry words. I was shocked and Connor was stunned. Leaning as far back as he could without falling out of the window, his face was white and his eyes were wide. My face was red and my eyes gushed with tears. We were at a painful crossroads. In that split-second I *felt* little difference between what had happened ten years earlier, on my mother-in-law's lawn, and Connor's desire to play war. Both had guns as central features, both involved power struggles and displays of violence, and both were out of my control. My emotional reaction sprang from the same well — I'm ultimately out of control over anyone but myself.

Throughout history kids have "played" their way through battles and wars. Researchers, historians, sociologists, and psychologists explain this as part of a child's attempt to master the concepts of power, conflict, and resolution. In moments such as this, however, no descriptions help. My brother-in-law Dave (married to my husband's sister) had no history of violent behavior, and yet shot his way into my mother-in-law Margaret's home, killing his wife, Laura, and their three young daughters before throwing the gun down at Margaret's feet and taunting her to pick it up and kill him. She was there with him for thirty minutes before any help arrived. Margaret lived the rest of her life from a place of deep woundedness and trauma. As her caregiver for these remaining years, I saw, firsthand, how guns can take and impact lives.

While Connor had only been two at the time of the murders, he had grown up knowing how his aunt and cousins died—knowing how I felt about guns. It was not a nebulous issue. I was opposed and firmly believed that comfort with any kind of gun was unnecessary. He, however, felt he could hold on to a pacifistic worldview and still "play" with toy guns. He hadn't played with them at all as a young child but now he was twelve and, while he was incredibly sensitive about relationships, highly compliant, and very loving, he never manifested concern about my feelings surrounding guns. In this moment, with his mom yelling at him across the van's front seat, he no longer had the luxury of disregarding my feelings. They were bold and loud and in his face.

I pulled over. I got a hold of myself. We talked.

At root, the murders had forever changed me. They'd made crystal clear the point that I ultimately had very little control of the events shaping my life. They demonstrated that loving people is risky and that, sometimes, those you love will make choices influencing their lives and the lives of others in profound and painful ways. The violent deaths had served to focus my fear and expand my sadness. I could never again say "that will never happen to me" in relation to the reality of physical violence, in my own family or elsewhere.

During my roadside encounter with Connor, though, I came face-to-face with the reality that his experience was just that. His. Connor's. While we may have shared a home, a lifestyle, and even, for a period of time, a body, we remained, uniquely, our own people. We agreed on some issues and differed wildly on others. He did not belong to me or have a lifetime subscription to my values and ideals. He was fully his own person, with his own independent thoughts, beliefs, and experiences. This realization has turned out to be the hardest reality of parenting for me.

I have attempted to assure myself that Connor's upbringing will lead him to an adulthood filled with meaning, intention, and integrity, infused with expressions of grace, love, and empathy. In doing so, I have at times tried to tell myself that I must make sure he believes certain things, ascribes to certain values, and is far beyond being "normal." Normal twelve-year-old boys, however, are intrigued by guns. Normal twelve-year-old boys are easily influenced by an object-obsessed culture. My son is intrigued by guns. My son wants new things. My son is normal!

While this realization should have been a relief, it hit me as a disappointment. Since his birth I had been happy to discover the many ways in which Connor was *not* normal. His strong relational bent set him apart from his same-age male counterparts. His early and advanced language skills supported his drive to connect. He loved to entertain and took pains to do so. He was aware of spiritual things and also of the temperament and preferences of others. He was smart and capable and, if I had anything to say about it, not normal.

I didn't want to be normal either. I wanted to be the informed mom. The "oh-it's-no-sweat-setting-boundaries-plus-giving-all-the-grace-and-love-possible" mom. The mom who raised a nontraditional boy. I was convinced that, if I was such a mom, the outcome would be a boy who was confident and strong and not macho or violent. The result, in my imagination, would be a boy who does not play with guns. Ever.

The problem, however, was that in my attempts to buck gender and evaluative stereotypes, I unconsciously told myself that if Connor showed any traditional "boy" traits, I had failed at the job of parenting. I had convinced myself that I could control Connor's interests, passions, and behaviors; that I knew what was best and most healthy for him; and that the ultimate goal of his life should be extreme excellence and maturity *by my standards at all times*. Each time this proved not true, I felt increasingly out of control, like a failure, and convinced all was not well in the world of our mother-son connectedness. As a therapist I piled on the self-doubt, fear, and condemnation, telling myself that if things were amiss within this connectedness, Connor would certainly fail to thrive outside of it. But somehow, armed with my psychological knowledge and teeth-gritting determination, I have been able to partner with my husband and God to parent Connor in such a way that Conner is emerging from the nest free from much of the unhealthy striving and concern about the opinion and approval of others that has plagued me.

In fact, my son has shown himself to be thoughtful about his actions, teachable, and appropriately confident in ways that I am not. He can stomach my disapproval of the games he plays with toy guns, he is willing to listen to my curiosity about how he can square his self-asserted pacifistic ideals with these games, and he's confident that he can live as a dedicated-to-peace man and still airsoft in the backyard with friends for an hour every few months. He takes stands about things he thinks are important. He is active in pursuits that expose and attempt to eradicate human trafficking. He quit playing video games that involve any violent content because he believes they are created by an industry that too powerfully affects young people. While I don't understand how he can take these strong stances while still shooting his friends with an airsoft gun, it's not up to me to make these decisions for him. That reality makes me crazy.

Letting go of my deeply dredged desire to control my children is difficult on good days and impossible on hard ones. It involves me coming to terms with my own lack of power and acknowledging the reality that it is neither fair nor realistic for me to measure my parenting success or personal prowess by my children's behaviors, beliefs, or moral standing. Neither can I force them to take on the values and standards I believe to be in their best interests. My striving to teach, to expose, to mirror, and to empathize is just that: mine. Their desire to take what I offer, to shape their own behavior, intelligence, and values are just that: theirs. I can structure and shape their experiences to a point. I can educate and share resources and personal knowledge. I can build a community of support for them to reference when I am not who they want. I can put child locks on the knife drawers and "play with me" signs on the Fisher Price doctor kit, but I cannot control the inner workings of my children's motivational selves or temperaments.

As I write this, the increasingly outspoken pacifist, seventeen-year-old Connor and his all-sides-of-the-table friends are out back, playing with their airsoft guns. These young men, confident, deep in faith, and rich in intelligence, are the exploring, work-in-progress young men they are supposed to be. Their laughter is infectious and this game is but a game—not my game but theirs, only one tiny activity in their arsenal of many. I don't endorse it, but I deeply endorse them. I don't like I, but I deeply love them. This love is risky and engaging and requires me to give up control at appropriate times and in measured increments. Doing so hurts and heals, challenges, and fulfills. What more could I ask of this crazy, complicated, conflict-inherent process called mothering?

Nothing.

Starbucks-colored Glasses

Lisa Graham McMinn

Lisa Graham McMinn, mother of three daughters and the grandmother of two granddaughters, is a professor of sociology at George Fox University. She lives on Fern Creek, a small farm outside of Newberg, Oregon, where she and her husband, Mark, run a small-scale CSA, tending chickens, bees, vegetables, berries, and a small orchard. Besides teaching and farming, Lisa enjoys reading and writing. Her books include *Growing Strong Daughters* (Baker, 2007), *The Contented Soul* (InterVarsity Press, 2006) and *Walking Gently on the Earth* (InterVarsity Press, 2010). Readers can find her reflections on life, love, and farming at www.ferncreekfarm.us.

SARAH, my middle school daughter, finished her hot chocolate as I licked the last bit of foam from my mocha. We returned the white mugs to the counter and started our walk home. Glen Ellyn, the suburb next door, sits less than a mile from our house in Wheaton and is one of the wealthiest suburbs of Chicago.

In 1996, it also held the nearest Starbucks.

Wheaton ranks high on the affluent scale, too, and Mark and I found raising our daughters in Chicago's wealthy western suburbs a challenge. Our neighborhood, like most others, displayed well-landscaped front yards conspicuously absent of garden gnomes, plastic lawn chairs, and kiddy pools. It sounded like everyone our children knew went to the Bahamas or France for vacation and drove BMWs when they weren't driving decked-out minivans. Maids cleaned houses and landscape services kept lawns cut, fertilized, and weed-free. We wondered how we would teach mindfulness and care for marginalized people when we didn't see or rub shoulders with anyone in our neighborhood who seemed disadvantaged.

None of that was on our mind when we originally relocated our family to Wheaton, where Mark had accepted a teaching position at Wheaton College. We wanted our three elementary and middle school daughters to fit in. So we took them shopping for new clothes, got them new haircuts, ended our geeky family bike rides and, well, started taking them on coffee dates to Starbucks.

I would be a hip mother, not a hick who embarrassed them.

Two men in business suits headed out of the Starbucks at the same time Sarah and I did, carrying their coffee to go. They politely opened the door for us, nodded, and smiled as we walked out. We passed an older, disheveled woman sitting on a bench outside of Starbucks, hunched over a graying canvas bag stuffed (presumably) with her few personal belongings. It surprised me a fair bit to see her sitting there — grossly out of place on the otherwise tidy and quaint storefront sidewalk. I didn't meet her gaze, but in case she was looking at me I tossed a nod and a smile her direction as Sarah and I began our walk home.

Sarah's eyes were on me, as daughters' eyes are often on their mothers, wondering how I would respond to the unusual sight of an apparently homeless woman in Glen Ellyn. I felt a nudging to turn around and speak to the woman, but shrugged it off. I didn't know what I'd say anyway.

But then I heard one of the business-suit-clad men berating the woman for being dirty and lazy. Why didn't she get a job? Didn't she care that she was hurting Starbucks's business by keeping customers away with her presence? Go to a shelter. Take a bath for Christ's sake.

The man's sharp, belittling tone got our attention. We stopped to offer a watchful eye, fearful now for the woman. She kept her eyes downcast as the tirade continued. I said to Sarah, "We should go back." She nodded, likely as unsure of what "going back" would entail as I. The men moved on, though I'd like to hope they saw us returning and felt jolted into some remorse.

The woman stood now, getting ready to move on, fearful perhaps that the men would return with police officers, or that we, emboldened by the men, had come to offer more of the same.

"I'm sorry that happened to you," I said. "He shouldn't have talked to you that way."

She looked up and met my gaze, and looked over at Sarah. "It's okay, but thank you. That means a lot to me."

We talked for a few minutes. I remember little about the conversation except that her name was Sherry, and that she spent the summers mostly meandering around Glen Ellyn. She said "God bless you" a lot. And also that Starbucks was nice, because most of its employees let her in to use the bathroom.

During our walk home, Sarah wondered if maybe we should invite her to live with us, and I squirmed at the suggestion. We decided to take dinner to her that night, my concession to offering her something more robust. We drove back an hour later with a bagel sandwich, a cheese stick, a couple of Mark's homemade snickerdoodle cookies, and an apple.

She looked in the bag and said, "God bless you. Thank you. Your kindness means so much." She rummaged through the bag and still looking into the bag said, "You're so kind... but...I can't eat bagels and apples....My teeth...." And then I noticed that she was missing a number of them and felt foolish for not thinking about this earlier. "Your kindness, it means a lot to me," she repeated, perhaps fearing she had offended us.

We returned weekly with sack suppers (replacing bagels and apples with sandwiches and yogurt) throughout the rest of the summer and fall, sometimes finding her and sometimes not. Early on we asked about her family. Sherry had a daughter, but became elusive when talking about her. "It's not good for me to live with her," she said, looking at her feet. "Besides, I like living on the street, especially in the summertime." Once she asked if we'd drive her up to the drug store where she could buy cigarettes: We did. Always we wished her well; she blessed us, telling us how much our kindness meant to her.

As the weather turned we noticed that a community of people had rallied around Sherry. She had a new blanket one week, a sweater another. When we asked what she needed she said, "Warm socks would be nice. Otherwise I have all I need." So we brought her socks, and the next week she said it would be nice to have some sort of organized transportation once the weather got cold. The churches that offered shelter and dinner could be up to seven miles apart and the homeless folk had to walk there themselves. "It's not so hard on the young ones, but my feet aren't so good anymore. A shuttle would be nice," she said.

I wish I had taken on the challenge to look into getting a shuttle, but I let her request go. She asked for something I didn't know how to give—and, perhaps, a role I didn't want to take on. I wanted to believe I had contributed what I could, and that some other more capable soul would take on the shuttling task. One week in October we didn't see her anymore, and while we went back a few more times, we never saw her again. Often I wondered what became of her.

I haven't thought much, recently, about those three months or so, and Sarah and I haven't talked about Sherry for years. Yet Sarah remains a compassionate soul with eyes to see the invisible and marginalized better than I do. She went on to college and then culinary school, majoring in art with a Third-World development minor. Currently Sarah works as the baker for an upscale restaurant and has dreams of eventually being her own boss. She has spent a number of years working in various capacities in food service, an industry notorious for treating workers like expendable parts. Sarah, like most kitchen employees, works full time yet receives no benefits, no paid vacation, and her employer has found a legal way to avoid paying her for overtime.

Over Sarah's years working in the food industry she has seen employers take advantage of the limited options of immigrants, the ignorance of high school dropouts, and the desperation of people caught in cycles of poverty. But she has also witnessed what is possible. In Grand Rapids, Michigan, she worked at Marie Catrib's, a restaurant owned by Marie, an immigrant herself, who experienced the challenges and indignities confronting immigrant workers, and now runs a highly successful business that respects workers, pays them well, and treats them with dignity.

Sarah will not be at her current job for long, although few people quit such positions. The economy and the competitive nature of work in the food industry reinforce the hold that employers have over employees. But Sarah will remember this experience, and when she moves on, she never wants to take her credentials, education, or connections for granted.

Recently, Sarah called to talk through anger and frustration at not receiving the overtime pay she expected after agreeing to work nine-hour days and to give up one of her days off to help out during a crisis. Then, in the midst of her teary frustration, she spoke words of deep empathy that harkened me back to that tidy street in front of a Glen Ellyn Starbucks. Sarah described how she welcomed the hardness of this experience, wanting the frustration to seep deep into her bones, allowing her the opportunity to show solidarity with others whose desperation, limited options, and relative powerlessness make them easy to exploit.

Sarah has the ability to see through her own personal troubles to bigger social issues about how we, as individuals and a society, treat the invisible living and working among us: bakers at our local restaurants, janitors and maids who clean our places of employment and sometimes our homes, clerks at department and grocery stores, field laborers, dish washers and kitchen hands. These are people who, like the homeless woman outside of Starbucks, deserve to be treated with dignity. People who, like the homeless woman, deserve to be seen. Sarah's willingness to truly see these people and have compassion for them moves me to tears.

Breinigsville, PA USA
18 March 2011
257950BV00004B/3/P